Activities for Public Sector Training: Achieving Change and Strengthening Teamwork

Activities for Public Sector Training: Achieving Change and Strengthening Teamwork

Edited by
Mary Griffiths

Gower

Published by
Gower Publishing Limited
Gower House
Croft Road
Aldershot
Hampshire GU11 3HR
England

Gower
Old Post Road
Brookfield
Vermont 05036
USA

British Library Cataloguing in Publication Data
Activities for Public Sector Training:
Achieving Change and Strengthening Teamwork
  I. Griffiths, Mary
  658.3124

ISBN 0–566–07651–9

Typeset in New Baskerville by Poole Typesetting (Wessex) Ltd, Bournemouth and printed in Great Britain by A. Rowe Ltd, Chippenham.

Contents

Contents

Part II   Change management skills

Part III   Improving team and individual performance

Appendixes

Preface

Like most trainers working in public sector organizations I have spent many hours searching for suitable training activities or rewriting and modifying activities designed for those working in a private sector environment.

There are numerous similarities between private sector and public sector work – trainers and staff from both kinds of organization share many problems and frequently deal with almost identical working situations. However, there are also significant differences in the nature of the work, the working context and the culture of the organizations concerned. These differences can make training activities designed for one type of organization difficult to use in another. For this reason I was asked to select and edit a collection of Gower training activities to meet the needs and working styles of public sector trainers and managers.

The activities in this manual are drawn from earlier Gower volumes and have been modified for inclusion in this collection. I would like to thank the authors of these exercises for allowing me to use and adapt their work.

In selecting the activities I have confined myself to two broad themes – the implementation of change and the need to strengthen and maintain team and individual performance in a more demanding and increasingly competitive working environment. These issues are priorities for today's public sector managers. The volume also includes some activities focused on the skills needed to manage change and performance – for example, communication, counselling, influencing and negotiation.

All the activities could be run by a trainer or facilitator working with a mixed course group or with an established working team. Many of them could also be used by managers or team leaders working with their own staff group. In every case I would advise the trainer or manager to prepare for the activity by:

● Carefully reading and thinking through the activity and its objectives.

- Ensuring that you have a sufficient knowledge of the underlying theory.

- Ensuring that you are fully aware of the needs of participants.

It is good practice to try out an exercise in advance wherever possible – especially if you have limited experience of running this type of exercise. This will give you the opportunity to decide if you wish to modify the activity or materials to meet the particular needs of your own situation.

I wish you every success with these activities and hope that you and the participants working with you find them both rewarding and enjoyable.

Mary Griffiths

A note on sources

The material in this manual is based on activities drawn as follows from volumes previously published by Gower/Connaught Training.

Activities for Achieving Change, by Barry Fletcher with Ann Bell, John Buttery and Mike Whittaker.
Activities 1, 2, 3, 4, 5, 9, 10, 11, 12, 16, 21, 32 and 34.

Role Plays for Developing Management Skills by Di Kamp.
Activities 8 and 14.

Activities for Achieving Managerial Effectiveness by Terry Wilson.
Activities 6, 7, 31, 33, 35 and 40.

50 Activities for Developing Management Skills Volume 5 by Simon James.
Activities 13, 20, 22, 23, 24, 29, 30, 36 and 39 and Appendix A.

Activities for Developing Appraisal Training by Wendy Denham and Jane Jestico.
Activities 25, 27, 28, 37 and 38.

50 Activities for Developing Counselling Skills by Roy Bailey.
Activities 15, 17, 18, 19 and 26.

50 Activities for Developing Management Skills Volume 1 by Leslie Rae.
Appendix B.

Symbols

Handout sheet

OHP transparency master

Cut up as indicated

Trainer's material

Index to activities

Activity no. Activity title	Page no.	Change	Self-awareness development	Managing stress	Organizational change	Developing the team	Quality of service	Communication	Planning	Creativity	Problem solving	Consultancy	Influencing	Negotiating	Constructive confrontation	Counselling	Meetings	Writing skills	Targets and standards
1 Turning crisis into opportunity	3	●	●	●	●	●													
2 Understanding reaction to change	7	●	●	●	●	●		●											
3 Adjusting to the phases of transition	21	●	●	●				●											
4 Heightening awareness of organizational culture	27	●	●		●	●	●	●											
5 Influencing organizational culture	35	●			●	●	●	●					●						
6 Working climate survey	45	●	●		●	●	●	●											
7 Operation improvement	59	●					●	●					●						
8 Making changes	73	●				●		●		●	●	●	●	●	●		●		
9 Opting for green	83	●			●	●	●	●		●	●								
10 Shifting our attitudes to service	87	●				●	●		●		●								
11 Building my consultancy style	95	●	●					●			●	●	●						
12 Triggering my ability to influence others	105	●	●					●				●	●	●					
13 First-class travel	111	●						●	●		●		●	●	●		●		
14 Excuses, excuses	121	●	●			●		●	●		●		●	●	●			●	●
15 Constructive confrontation	129	●					●	●			●		●	●	●	●			
16 Enhancing my counselling approach	135	●	●					●			●					●			
17 Counselling empathy scale	145	●	●					●			●					●			
18 Combining counselling skills	153	●	●					●			●				●	●			
19 Going for goals	163	●			●	●		●	●	●	●			●	●		●		●
20 Fishbone that problem	169	●			●	●			●	●	●								
21 Reducing harmful stress	175	●	●		●			●	●										
22 Agenda	183	●				●		●									●		
23 Brief moments	187	●						●									●		
24 The message was …	193	●						●											
25 Just stick to the facts	203	●						●	●		●				●				
26 Is anybody listening?	207	●	●					●				●	●			●	●		
27 Let me explain	211	●						●										●	
28 Easy listening	215	●	●					●					●		●	●	●		
29 The glass of life	221	●							●		●								
30 Communication charter	233	●				●		●	●		●								
31 From group to team	241					●		●									●		
32 Developing team goals	247	●				●					●		●	●	●				●
33 Team characteristics	257					●		●	●		●				●				
34 Introducing new patterns of work	267	●			●	●	●	●	●	●	●		●	●	●				●
35 Team process analysis	277					●		●	●		●				●				
36 Postal dilemma	283					●		●		●	●								
37 For better or verse	293	●					●	●	●									●	●
38 Bullseye	299	●					●	●	●									●	●
39 Ghostbusters	309	●				●		●	●		●			●	●	●			
40 Your team leader role	313	●	●	●															

Time checklist

This checklist indicates the minimum time to be allocated to each activity. Times will be affected by the number of participants and whether or not a limit is set on discussion periods.

Up to one hour

24   The message was …

25   Just stick to the facts

26   Is anybody listening?

27   Let me explain

31   From group to team

37   For better or verse

41   Questions I'd like to ask

42   Activity appraisal

Between one and two hours

8   Making changes

9   Opting for green

12   Triggering my ability to influence others

13   First-class travel

14   Excuses, excuses

Between two and three hours

Over three hours

Part I
The challenge of change

1

Turning crisis into opportunity

Description

This is an activity which examines emotional reaction to a crisis, identifies the opportunities presented and creates a constructive action plan.

Situations

This activity can be used for an organizational problem which at the outset appears to be a crisis. Examples might be:

- Closure of a service unit or section.
- Restructuring of a department, section or service.
- Requirement to reduce staffing levels.
- Putting a service out to tender.
- Loss of a contract.
- A strike, or other form of industrial action.
- The introduction of an imposed change to established methods of working.

Alternatively, this activity could be adapted to a crisis faced by an individual. The process would be slightly different and the steps are outlined under Method. In such cases support for the individual experiencing the crisis would come from another person (the manager or possibly the trainer in some situations) rather than a group.

Objectives

- To provide an opportunity for release and expression of emotions at a time of crisis.

- To acknowledge the positive aspects of change which can arise from difficult situations.

- To identify difficulties/obstacles facing the group/individual.

- To produce an action plan 'in defiance of' the crisis.

Trainer guidance

Your principal role is as a facilitator. You should encourage trust and openness, particularly in the early stages of the activity when a willingness to express real feelings will contribute to the process of making changes happen in what could be difficult and even traumatic circumstances.

Method

WORKING WITH A GROUP

1. *Crisis definition.* Working with participants, define the crisis. This should result in an unambiguous statement written on a flipchart, or similar aid, which concentrates on the problem itself rather than why it has occurred.

2. *Summary of feelings.* Divide participants into pairs or small groups and ask them to discuss their emotional response to the crisis. It is important that both negative and positive feelings are aired. Use prompts such as:

   - What does this situation mean to *you?*
   - What are the words which express your feelings?
   - How did you feel when first faced with this crisis?
   - How do you feel at this moment?

   Bring participants together and produce a list of key words which cover the range of emotions, displaying them on a flipchart. Allow time for discussion to explore different individual reactions.

3. *Definition of the qualities of the team.* This stage begins to translate feelings into positive action. Typical statements could be:

   - OK to have negative feelings initially.
   - The 'crisis' may present opportunities to the individual and the team.

4

- Focusing on the positive helps the team to move away from the crisis.

Ask participants to return to their pairs or small groups to summarize the strengths of each participant.

This stage is working towards the conclusion that: 'We may feel downcast but now we have thought about it there is much we can contribute to this crisis situation.'

4. *Brainstorm the 'crisis'.* Bring together participants and remind them of the statement agreed at step 1. Ask them to suggest as many ideas as they can relative to the 'crisis', all of which are recorded without discussion. These can then be categorized into 'very useful' or 'potentially useful'.

5. *Review of the options.* Making use of the material from the brainstorming session, discuss the options open to the participants to arrive at:

   (a) Our most favoured course of action is ...
   (b) The course of action we find acceptable is ...
   (c) Our least favoured course of action (but still just acceptable) is ...

6. *Agreement on course of action.* Produce an action plan in the form of a statement which details:

   - Who is to do what.
   - When.
   - How.
   - Resources required.
   - Who can provide support and assistance.
   - Means of evaluation.

7. *Evaluation of 'crisis exercise'.* Evaluation reactions to the activity:

   - What have we learned?
   - What might we use again?
   - What do we now think about a 'crisis'?

WORKING WITH AN INDIVIDUAL

The steps are similar and should be followed as above, taking into consideration the following:

1. Work with a partner to clarify the 'crisis' and explore feelings.

2. Identify individual qualities and strengths and discuss with a partner.

3. Share key questions with a partner. For example:

   - What are my options?
   - What are some of the limiting factors?
   - Who can give me support?

5

4. Produce a personal action plan which can be 'contracted' with a partner.

5. Periodic review of the action plan.

Timing

1. Crisis definition takes thirty minutes.

2. Summary of feelings takes one hour.

3. Qualities of the team takes one hour.

4. Brainstorming takes thirty minutes.

5. Review of options takes one hour.

6. Agreement on course of action takes one hour.

7. Evaluation takes thirty minutes.

Average total time: five to six hours.

These times are for working with a group. For individual work the process may take several sessions spread over a period of time.

Materials required

1. Flipcharts, paper and pens.

2. Sufficient space to work undisturbed.

2

Understanding reaction to change

Description

This activity uses a case study to help participants reflect upon and discuss practical procedures for dealing with reactions to organizational change.

Situations

Suitable in the training of managers and supervisors who are faced with the prospect of significant organizational change.

Objectives

- To appreciate the possible outcomes of introducing change.
- To reduce change to identifiable component parts.
- To gauge the likely reaction to each of the change components.
- To consider strategies for minimizing resistance to organizational change within the case study.
- To take decisions about transferring learning to the workplace.

Trainer guidance

This activity has been designed to enable managers/supervisors to consider the process of organizational change and to reflect upon ways of attaining improved levels of acceptance. You may wish to refer to the trainer's notes

(Handout 2.1) which provide useful background information to this activity. As part of the group's preparation you may choose to send each participant Handout 2.1, together with copies of the case study, Document 2.4, one to two weeks before the activity.

Method

1. Give a brief introduction and overview of the subject, using, if necessary, the trainer's notes (Handout 2.1).

2. Give a copy of Handout 2.2 to each participant and briefly explain its use (that is, an analytical instrument which can be used to assist in the evaluation of a specific organizational change with the aim of developing a strategy for acceptance).

    As an option, participants can be taken through the steps in Handout 2.3 to increase understanding of their use of the form. At each stage, ask participants to contribute their own views, share them with colleagues and ask questions before moving on.

3. Distribute Handout 2.4. Divide participants into groups of three to five participants and ask each group to proceed through the following stages:

    (a) Analyse the case study with the aid of Handout 2.2.
    (b) Decide upon a strategy aimed at minimizing resistance to change.
    (c) Prepare to report on the chosen strategy.

4. Allow time for groups to present their strategies to the main group. Encourage discussion, challenges and questions.

5. In the main group hold a learning review session, addressing questions such as:

    ● How valuable is this structured approach?
    ● Which current and anticipated changes lend themselves to this approach?
    ● What obstacles are anticipated in using this approach and how will they be circumvented?

Conclude by asking participants to give examples of how, where and when they intend to use this approach in the near future.

Timing

1. The introduction/overview takes twenty to thirty minutes.

2. Explaining Handout 2.2 takes ten minutes and working through Handout 2.2 (optional) takes forty minutes.

3. Strategy choice takes forty-five to sixty minutes.

4. Presentations/discussion takes fifteen minutes.

5. Learning review/application takes twenty minutes.

Average total time with three groups: three hours.

Materials required

1. Sufficient copies of Handouts 2.1, 2.2, 2.3 and 2.4.

2. Sufficient space for groups to work undisturbed.

3. Flipchart, paper, OHP acetates and pens for presentations.

Understanding reaction to change – trainer's notes

Managers, supervisors and other people are often faced with the challenge of introducing change. This can be:

(a) *self-created* – the idea, the resources and the authority to make it happen; or

(b) *imposed* – variable influence plus responsibility for implementing change with minimum disruption to operations.

The change could be large-scale and even drastic, as in the case of major restructuring or loss of a contract to external contractors with redundancies. At the other extreme, the change could be subtle or slight, as in the case of a minor change to a job description.

Typical change situations

- Restructuring of the organization.

- Contracting out of services.

- Introduction of new technology.

- Introduction of new systems, policies, procedures and practices.

- Increased levels of responsibility.

- Changes in duties.

- Increased levels of work or work pressure.

- Changes in the grading of posts or the introduction of performance-related pay.

Reactions to such changes can be considered as:

(a) *positive* – general agreement and acceptance by all concerned with their full commitment to making it happen; or

(b) *negative* – resistance to change for whatever reason.

The leader's task is to secure a positive reaction to the change. This may not come readily or easily but with foresight and careful planning a satisfactory outcome is possible.

11

Reflecting for a moment on the 'undesirable outcome', that is, a negative reaction or resistance, common causes are:

- Fear of the unknown.

- Sudden announcements of change without warning.

- Being pressurized into situations where unforeseen difficulties may arise.

- Many subtle and gradual changes over a long period, each of which is insignificant in isolation but taken as a whole can build up to frustration and even anger.

- No perception of gain, reward or service improvement, *or* perception of loss or reduced standards of service.

Some effects of resistance

- Drop in morale and motivation.

- An increase in conflict between members of teams.

- Reduced output.

- A drop in quality and standards of work.

- Refusal to cooperate and challenges to managers, even on issues unrelated to change.

- Increased absenteeism.

- Deterioration in time-keeping standards.

- Increased aggression in meetings.

Such effects can become key indicators of a change being resisted. Reaction to change can be anything from absolute refusal to cooperate at one extreme to full acceptance and commitment at the other. There are shades of resistance in between, for example:

(a) *hidden resistance* – individual or group acceptance but quiet striving towards causing a failed outcome;

(b) *cautious acceptance* – acceptance without full commitment, plus readiness to revert to resistance should problems occur.

Reproduced from *Activities for Public Sector Training: Achieving Change and Strengthening Teamwork,*
Gower Publishing Ltd.

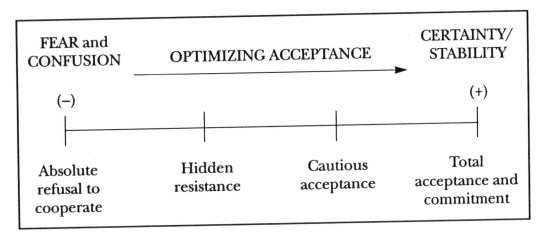

Scale of reaction

Whether the proposed change is imposed or self-created the leader will need to draft a strategy which will optimize acceptance. There will be a 'gap' between what is current and what is required. The aim is to close that gap as painlessly and effectively as possible.

Strategy for high acceptance

1. *Think* carefully and write down precisely the planned change.

2. *Consider* who will be affected most – directly and indirectly.

3. *Decide* what new skills and knowledge will be required for:

   - New policies and procedures.
   - New equipment and machinery.
   - Coping with related changes and tasks.
   - Coping with new working relationships.
   - Working within a new culture and/or environment.

4. *Determine* what existing knowledge can be used with this change.

5. *Decide* how best to communicate the change, for example:

   - Draft the change plan.
   - Discuss and clarify the purpose of the change with all concerned (may result in feedback showing likely reaction).
   - Seek suggestions but *do not* promise to follow them.
   - Make it clear that some staff may already have the knowledge and skills needed and that you will be asking for their support.
   - Use every opportunity to 'affirm' the change via memos, update meetings, newsletters, staff visits to other organizations or sections, circulation of journals, reports or other relevant materials etc.

- Design and communicate the training and coaching plan.
- Programme regular reviews.

6. *Establish* an 'acid test' for the change by asking yourself: 'How will I know that acceptance and commitment have been secured and the change achieved?'

Managing change – evaluation form

Complete the form below, using the instructions on the next sheet.

MANAGING CHANGE – EVALUATION FORM

a The change:						
b Change element	*c* Value	*d* Scale of reaction				*e* Why resistance?	*f* Benefits of the change
		A	B	C	D		To the organization	To the individual/group

15

Evaluation form – instructions for use

The letters relate to those which appear on the form.

b   Write down the actions which need to be taken to close the 'gap' between what is current and what is wanted.

c   To indicate 'value' use the following:

   V = Vital to success.
   B = Beneficial to quality of success.
   N = Neutral – makes no difference.

d   Tick in the appropriate box:

   A = absolute refusal to cooperate
   B = hidden resistance.
   C = cautious acceptance.
   D = full acceptance and commitment.

b–f   Use this evaluation to help you to formulate an outline strategy for success as follows:

Outline strategy for success

Develop the key strategy elements, utilizing the information from the form, which will be required for success. Consider:

- those affected (directly/indirectly)
- skills/knowledge required
- existing skills/knowledge which can be utilized
- how best to communicate the change.

ACID TEST

How will you know you have achieved success?

16

Example of use of Handout 2.2

The following example of introducing a new performance-related payment scheme increases understanding of using the form in Handout 2.2. The letters correspond to sections on the form.

a   Write down in a *single statement* the desired change. For example: 'To introduce a performance-related payment system based on annual targets.'

b   List those *key* change elements which will have to be actioned to effect the change successfully: that is, those actions which must be taken in order to close the gap between what is current and what is wanted.

       For this example, the following actions could be required:

- Engage a performance-related pay specialist.
- Set up a consultation process.
- Decide upon a department or staff group to be studied.
- Carry out pilot studies, using a model scheme.
- Establish the basis for measuring performance.
- Establish the financial basis of the scheme.
- Set up a monitoring system.

c   Judge the value of each element in turn for the success of implementation using the following codes:

    V = Vital. The change cannot be implemented without this being achieved.

    B = Beneficial. The change could be effected without this element being achieved but its absence will reduce the overall quality of the change.

    N = Neutral. Absence of this element will not affect the quality of the change. Use of this raises the question of whether it is 'key'.

d   Taking each element in turn, indicate on the 'scale of reaction' the likely reaction of the target group, where:

    A = absolute refusal to cooperate.
    B = hidden resistance.
    C = cautious acceptance.
    D = full acceptance and commitment.

e   In the event of resistance being anticipated, briefly state why.

f   List the main benefits to the organization, and to the individual or group, resulting from successful implementation of the change.

To conclude, invite participants to comment on:

- Their perception of the value of the form.
- Ease/difficulty in completing the form.
- Thoughts on applying the form to work situations.

Case study – understanding reaction to change

Organization X is a large public sector organization providing a wide range of services to the public. The organization has been going through a period of large-scale change which has involved a significant programme of compulsory competitive tendering and the introduction of extensive business planning systems. Even departments not immediately affected by competitive tendering are now establishing more commercial ways of working by negotiating service-level agreements with other parts of the organization using their services. These agreements specify the standard of service to be provided, the level/extent of service and the costs of the service. This involves a more precise approach to work and increased focus on standards and output than has been customary. There are also plans to introduce performance-related pay for senior staff throughout the organization. It is expected that this will be effective from the next financial year.

The problem

You are the manager of a new administrative services section providing information and routine clerical and office services to several other sections. You are required to fully integrate the section, which is a merger of two older sections, and to introduce new, more business-like ways of working which will support the introduction of service-level agreements and will facilitate the introduction of the performance-related pay scheme based on the achievement of annual targets. This scheme will apply to the ten most senior staff in the section.

The background to the administrative services section

The section has forty staff, ten at senior/supervisory level, ten specialist computer staff and twenty clerical and data input support staff. The section has only very recently been created and is formed from two older sections – information and clerical services. This merger was the result of full-scale reorganization which caused much anxiety and stress to the staff of both sections. Several people left on voluntary severance pay and the new section has still to sort out its routines and working methods.

The two older departments have very different staff groups with contrasting working styles and cultures.

19

The information staff are all men aged between eighteen and forty and all work full-time. Most of the work is technical and specialist and staff are highly motivated and committed to their work area. Gradings are high compared to those for staff in the rest of the organization and there is also a special arrangement for overtime payments above the standard rate. These arrangements reflect the problem of recruiting and retaining good staff in this field of work. During the reorganization there were three vacancies in the section – this prevented any anxiety about needing to reduce staff numbers.

The clerical services staff are predominantly women, aged between twenty-four and sixty. Twelve of them work on a part-time basis. Morale is low and sickness absence levels have risen significantly. The clerical services section had traditionally been poorly regarded in the section and staff have felt they did not have the resources or the training necessary to provide a good service. Most of the staff are on basic clerical grades and there is no paid overtime – except in very special circumstances. Six people left on voluntary severance pay during the reorganization; this ended a long period of anxiety when compulsory redundancy was feared.

Setting up the section to work effectively in the new climate will involve many changes. The most significant are:

- A review of grading and overtime arrangements.

- Establishing a system for recording the time taken on each piece of work, so that service users can be charged accordingly.

- Establishing standards for accuracy and output of work.

- Developing systems for monitoring standards.

- Increasing output.

- Introducing a system of performance targets for staff who will be moving on to the performance-related pay system.

3

Adjusting to the phases of transition

Description

This activity enables participants, with the help of others, to consider transition, that is, the passage from one place, state or stage to another. Opportunity is given for participants to consider the phases of transition against a background of personal change(s). Finally, participants are asked to think about options open to them in dealing with future transitions.

Situations

1. As an activity on a workshop which is considering aspects of stress.

2. Where individuals/groups in an organization are experiencing difficulty with change.

3. A component in any programme aimed at increasing self-awareness.

Objectives

- To examine the phases of transition in the light of personal examples shared by participants.

- To emphasize the positive aspects of transition and the help other people can provide in difficult times.

Trainer guidance

The concept of phases of transition is likely to be new to most participants and you will need to provide appropriate input. (Some background reading is recommended. For example: *Lifeskills Teaching Programmes No 1, 1980* and *No 2, 1982* by Barrie Hopson and Mike Scally, Lifeskills Associates, Leeds; and *Psychology for Managers*, edited by Cary Cooper and Peter Makin, The British Psychological Society, 1981, Chapter 7, written by Barrie Hopson.) As a facilitator, you will need to encourage openness and trust in the process of self-analysis and working in pairs. In the concluding session you will help to draw out learning points which may assist participants with future transitions.

Method

1. Introduce the following three forms of change and obtain examples of these from participants:

    (a) *Planned* – intended change, such as deciding on a career, changing jobs, moving house, getting married.
    (b) *Unplanned* – these may be unwanted by the individual, such as an accident, bereavement, restructuring of the work area, introduction of new methods of working or wanted, such as regrading of a post, promotion or a substantial bequest.
    (c) *Growing awareness* – the gradual realization that your life is changing, for example adolescence, approaching middle age, gaining or losing weight.

2. Discuss and explain to participants the basic theory of transition, that is, that the individual will experience a predictable cycle of reactions and feelings with a number of phases. Distribute Handout 3.1 which describes the seven phases.

    You can expect some debate on the phases of transition, for example the actual sequence. This confirms the uniqueness of each person's experience and the accompanying feelings. Participants may be unaware that in some cases something prevents them from getting beyond the 'minimization' or 'depression' stage.

3. Ask participants to select a recent or current personal transition and, working individually, write down their feelings. Use the following questions to prompt them:

    At the start:
    • What were my feelings?
    • How did I react at the time?
    • What helped and/or got in the way?

> *During:*   ● What was the range of feelings?
>   ● What techniques did I use to cope?
> *Now:*   ● What are my feelings at this moment?

4. Ask participants to form pairs and exchange ideas and feelings. They should concentrate on active listening and other behaviours which encourage openness.

5. Individually, ask participants to decide whether their transition is current or over. Use the following questions to help them decide.

> *Current:* ● What do I think will happen?
>   ● What do I really want to happen?
>   ● What can I learn from this?
> *Over:*   ● Did it work out as I wanted?
>   ● If not, why not?
>   ● What have I learned?

6. Ask participants to return to their original pairs and share their responses to step 5 above.

7. In pairs, ask each participant to explore and write down the individual learning he/she has gained from the exercise so far, together with the behaviours and actions which will help with any future transitions.

8. Hold a discussion with all the participants together, concentrating on what has been learned, rather than facts revealed in the discussion between pairs. It may be appropriate to explore the range of feelings experienced. The following conclusions may help to end the session on a positive note:

   ● The opportunity (presented by this activity) to express our feelings can help us over difficult times.
   ● Knowledge of the seven phases of transition may help us in dealing with future difficulties.
   ● Substantial problems and calamities can lead to personal growth.
   ● Other people are an important source of help in difficult times.
   ● We can also provide support to others.
   ● The situation may seem calamitous but most of the time we will cope.

Timing

1. The three forms of change takes fifteen minutes.

2. Discussion on transition takes thirty minutes.

3.–7. Individual/pair work takes on hour thirty minutes to two hours.*

8. Concluding discussion takes thirty minutes.

23

Average total time: three hours.

* Steps 3–7 may release some deep feelings among participants and additional time may be requested to progress this part to a satisfactory conclusion.

Materials required

1. Sufficient copies of Handout 3.1.
2. Flipchart, paper and pens.
3. Sufficient space and privacy for pairs to work undisturbed.

Transition

The seven phases of transition can be summarized as follows:

1. IMMOBILIZATION

A sense of being overwhelmed, unable to plan and understand. This may be particularly intense where the transition is apparently negative and totally unexpected, for example bereavement (close relative).

2. MINIMIZATION

A denial that the change exists. This has its positive side in that the situation may be too overwhelming to face head-on and time is thus provided to prepare for subsequent phases.

3. DEPRESSION

This feeling emerges from acknowledgement of the need to change apparently coupled with an initial feeling of powerlessness.

4. 'LETTING GO'

This is an acceptance of reality but with the knowledge 'I can survive'.

5. TESTING

In the new situation, different ways of coping are tried, sometimes accompanied by feelings of anger and irritability.

6. SEARCH FOR MEANING

After the energy of the 'Testing' phase this is the search for understanding how and why things are different.

7. INTERNALIZATION

Following on from an understanding of the transition, changes are incorporated in behaviour.

4

Heightening awareness of organizational culture

Among the many definitions of organizational culture, the following is one of the most useful:

> '... the deeper level of assumptions and beliefs that are shared by members of an organisation, that operate unconsciously and define in a basic "taken for granted" fashion an organisation's view of itself and its environment.' (Edgar Schein, *Organisational Culture and Leadership*, Jossey Bass, 1985)

Description

This activity is designed to open participants' eyes to the meaning of organizational culture and provide an opportunity for them to examine their own perceptions of culture within their own organization.

Situations

This activity is particularly useful for managers and supervisory staff – especially those who would benefit from a deeper understanding of what it is that makes their organization tick.

Objectives

- To describe the types of ingredient which make up an organization's culture.
- To list some key influences of culture.

- To pinpoint some aspects of organizational culture within participants' own organization.

- To consider the impact of this awareness on future behaviours.

Trainer guidance

You will need to be aware of organizational culture and its influence. Sensitivity to the politics of culture is important. You may benefit from some background reading and the work of Roger Harrison is recommended (*Understanding Your Organization's Culture*, Harrison Associates Inc., 1986).

Method

1. Starting with the term, 'The way we do things here', divide participants into small groups of three or four. Distribute Handout 4.1 and ask each group to discuss and record on a flipchart examples from their own experience which relate to some of the 'ingredients' of organizational culture as outlined in the handout. It may be appropriate to give each group some of the areas to avoid too much duplication during the feedback session.

2. Bring participants together and ask groups to share their statements and discuss. Explore participants' perceptions of the impact of culture in various areas, for example:

   - procedures;
   - behaviours;
   - attitudes, etc.

3. Distribute Handout 4.2 and ask participants to complete it individually, choosing their own organization, function, departmental or sectional focus.

   When participants have completed this, in pairs, ask them to share with each other their findings, with an overall aim of achieving maximum understanding of each other's view.

4. Bring participants together and ask them to decide and announce to the group their own conclusions on:

   - two or three points they have each learned about organizational culture;
   - how the session has made them think differently about the organization;
   - how each person has in the past knowingly/unknowingly helped/hindered the organization culture;

28

- how they believe their understanding can/may shape their future actions.

Timing

1. Recording statements takes thirty to forty minutes.

2. Sharing statements and discussion takes thirty minutes.

3. Completing Handout 4.2 and sharing in pairs takes thirty to forty minutes.

4. Review and conclusions takes thirty to forty minutes.

Average total time: two hours fifteen minutes.

Materials required

1. Sufficient copies of Handouts 4.1 and 4.2

2. Flipcharts and pens.

'Ingredients' of organizational culture

'Ingredients'	Examples
Rituals	• recognition for performance
	• treatment of new recruits
	• holidays
	• length of service
Myths	• stories of the past
	• stories about people
	• heroes and heroines
	• stories of successes/mistakes
Ceremonies	• meetings
	• addresses
	• celebrations
	• awards
Symbols	• car parking
	• eating arrangements
	• furnishings
	• titles
	• perks
Power	• sources of
	• recipients of
	• qualification for
	• visibility of
Systems	• communications
	• formal/informal
	• for promotion
	• place of paperwork
	• dealing with customers

'Tuning in' to organizational culture

Type of culture and examples of values and behaviours:	Comments and examples in my own organization:
Power • Hierarchical and authoritarian; dominated by strong leadership. • People strive for status, influence and proximity to 'power figures'. • Political skill is vital to personal progress. • Punishment and reward systems are in evidence, as is fear of failure. • Pleasing 'the boss' is an important concern; the leader is expected to be all-knowing and all-powerful. • Subordinates are expected to comply and often lack, or are denied, use of initiative. **Role** • Also hierarchical but power is exercised through the rules, systems and procedures. Leaders demand only what the system calls for. • People keep to defined duties and responsibilities – those who want to get on will 'do things right'! • Control and influence is achieved via impersonal exercise of power to enforce defined procedures and standards of performance. • Conflict suppressed by reference to 'the rules', procedures and definitions of responsibilities. • Order, rationality, formal channels and set procedures are evident.	

33

Type of culture and examples of values and behaviours:	Comments and examples in my own organization:
Achievement ● People share a common drive towards the achievement of valued goals and ideals. Staff are encouraged to use their talents and abilities in achieving goals to which they are personally committed. Motivation from inside 'the self' thus replaces external control through systems, rewards or punishment. ● Underlying assumption that people enjoy tasks which advance a shared purpose. A sense of passion and commitment to the work which can be deeply satisfying. ● High demands on people's time and energy can eventually lead to 'burn-out' and disillusion. **Support** ● Leaders are concerned with and respond to the personal needs and values of others; highly willing to provide development opportunities for staff. People are open to learning and both giving and receiving help. ● Staff are effective and competent in interpersonal relationships. Individuals are seen as interesting and worthwhile in their own right. Staff trust the organization to take care of them and in return, they take care of the organization. ● Tendency to avoid conflict in order to preserve harmony. Consensus may be overvalued to the detriment of speedy decision making.	

Note. Organizations are unlikely to display one single culture 'type'. However, there may be one dominant orientation together with elements of other 'types'.

34

5

Influencing organizational culture

Description

This thought-provoking activity allows participants to explore the mission of their organization (or of their part of the organization) and to identify those ingredients of organizational culture which are most desirable for the achievement of strategic goals. Differences between 'actual' and 'desirable' culture are highlighted and these are followed by proposals for change.

Situations

This activity is best suited to a coherent group within the organization, for example a senior management group representing all main functions (horizontal slice), a functional group (vertical slice) or a mixed-function group representing all levels (diagonal slice). However, it can be adapted for use with a mixed group representing several organizations or departments within a large organization. This would have the benefit of raising participants' awareness of differing organizational cultures.

However used, there should be a climate in which participants' views and suggestions will be listened to with interest and open-mindedness.

Objectives

- To identify the mission and strategic goals of the participant's organization or part of the organization.

- To form conclusions on 'desirable' culture.

- To contrast 'desirable' culture with 'actual'.

- To develop a case for changing aspects of culture.
- To produce a plan for change *or* a strategy for presenting a case.

Trainer guidance

When participants share their thoughts and opinions on organizational culture and suggestions for change, the quality of data generated depends on the degree of openness and trust which participants feel. In fact, the very culture which they are exploring may resist the activity! You will need to 'pave the way', where possible reducing apprehensions and any fear of recrimination, and helping participants to feel comfortable about sharing what they think and feel about their organization.

The process involves close examination of the way things are done now, moving on to how things might be done differently and what would be the benefits of changing. Your role is to work towards a climate where such discussion can take place: adhering to the objectives of the activity; defusing destructive and negative behaviours and encouraging participants to think creatively about desirable changes.

Where the activity includes presentations to senior managers you can assist greatly by arranging for these people to attend at the appropriate time; brief them to listen carefully to presentations; encourage them to ask questions; explain to them the importance of treating suggestions positively and being prepared to treat them as a valuable data in their decision-making processes.

Although the activity can be used on its own, you may like to lead into it through Activity 4 – Heightening awareness of organizational culture.

Method

1. Introduce the activity, emphasizing the value of openness and creative thinking throughout the process. Invite participants to arrive at statements which describe the organization's mission, that is, what the organization exists to do. If you prefer, you can focus this on the mission of a department or specific part of the organization. Supplement this with statements of the organization's key strategies, that is, how it intends to allocate its resources in order to achieve the mission. (Note: this step could be carried out in the main group or in smaller groups which then share and consolidate their findings.)

   Prompts which could help this step could include:

   - What is the organization's purpose?
   - What are its key goals?
   - How is the organization to interact with its environment?
   - How is it to interact with employees and others?

2. Divide participants into groups, distribute Handout 5.1 and brief them on the tasks. Distributing Handout 4.2 will also help participants with background definitions of the main types of organizational culture. Instruct groups to discuss and reach agreement on five main areas for change. Ask each group to prepare a short presentation of its findings.

3. Bring participants together and ask each group to present its suggestions for cultural change, together with anticipated benefits. Participants should ask questions, give constructive criticism and feedback. Hold a debate on the advantages of proposed changes over the current situation.

4. Instruct each group to carry out one of the following tasks (a or b):

    (a) Prepare a presentation on a strategy for change to be made to one or more senior managers who can influence organizational culture. Include in the presentation:

    ● Rationale.
    ● Gaps perceived between 'actual' and 'desirable' culture.
    ● Proposals for change.
    ● Benefits and advantages of the proposals.
    ● Suggestions for implementation.

    (b) Prepare a presentation, to be made to the main group, of a plan for achieving culture change. Include in the presentation:

    ● Specific changes to be made.
    ● Timescale of the plan.
    ● Responsibilities for implementation.
    ● Support and monitoring arrangements.

5. Bring participants together and allow time for presentations to be made. Participants should discuss each and ask questions. Where the presentation is to senior managers, ensure they contract clearly with the groups on the next steps.

6. In a plenary session, encourage discussion of the activity, sharing thoughts on the process and the learning which participants feel they have gained.

Timing

1. Introduction and forming the statements takes thirty to sixty minutes.

2. Completing Handout 5.1 and presentations takes forty-five to sixty minutes.

3. Sharing suggestions and debate takes sixty to ninety minutes.

4. Preparing presentations takes thirty to forty-five minutes.

5. Presentations take sixty to ninety minutes.

6. Plenary session takes twenty to thirty minutes.

Average total time: between one half and one full day, including breaks.

Materials required

1. Sufficient copies of Handouts 5.1 and 4.2.

2. Sufficient space for participants to work undisturbed.

3. Flipcharts, paper and pens.

Identifying desirable culture elements

Part 1

Against the background of organizational mission and key strategies, record your thoughts on 'desirable' ingredients of culture in the middle column. Ask yourself what values, practices and behaviours make most sense if the mission/strategies are to be accomplished. Please feel free to extend the 'ingredient areas' given and add those of your own choosing. Then complete the right-hand column to show your perception of the present situation.

Ingredient	'Desirable' values, practices and behaviours	'Actual' values, practices and behaviours
Rituals		
Myths		

39

Ingredient	'Desirable' values, practices and behaviours	'Actual' values, practices and behaviours
Ceremonies		
Symbols		
Power		

Ingredient	'Desirable' values, practices and behaviours	'Actual' values, practices and behaviours
Systems		

41

Ingredient	'Desirable' values, practices and behaviours	'Actual' values, practices and behaviours

Part 2

On the following scales, and using Handout 4.2 as background material, indicate your perception of the cultural mix within your organization. Place a 'D' at the appropriate point on each scale to indicate the desirable cultural mix for achievement of the organization's mission/key strategies. Place an 'A' on each scale to show what you believe to be the current position.

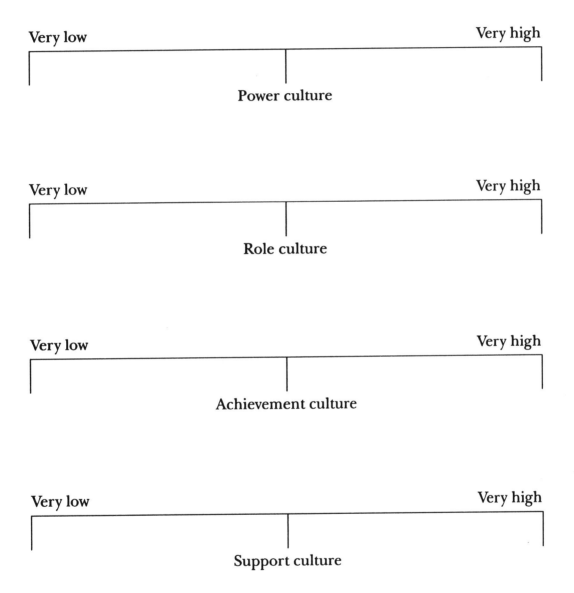

Very low   Very high

Power culture

Very low   Very high

Role culture

Very low   Very high

Achievement culture

Very low   Very high

Support culture

Part 3

From your work in Parts 1 and 2, identify the *five* biggest differences between 'desirable' and 'actual' culture. Rank these in order of importance to you and suggest possible ways of reducing the 'gaps' together with anticipated benefits.

Item	How to change	Anticipated benefits
1.		
2.		
3.		
4.		
5.		

6

Working climate survey

Description

This activity helps participants to assess the environment in their section or department and to develop an action plan aimed at building a more positive working climate.

Situations

The activity can be used in a variety of ways, depending on the composition of the training group. Examples might be:

- For individual managers to examine their styles and the climate they set with their team.

- For a group of managers from the same department to complete and analyse the results collectively.

The exercise is for groups of about six participants.

Objectives

- To identify the main factors affecting motivation in a working environment.

- To plan for improvement.

Trainer guidance

One well-known definition of management is 'the process of getting things done through people'. For this reason the climate and atmosphere that a manager creates will affect performance.

Managers require an understanding of what really motivates people so that they fully engage in their work, are committed and want to excel and do the best possible job. For many years there was a view that one set of factors motivated managers and a different set motivated others. We have learned that for many people in organizations this was an incorrect assumption. It has been generated by certain types of management thinking, views of people and organizations, and the type of technology introduced in organizations. These factors imposed strict limits on the amount of freedom, discretion and decision making allowed to the average working person. The result was that they could be fully functioning human beings out of work, capable of managing their families and other personal matters, while in work they were restricted to a very narrow band of activity and thinking.

In many organizations this thinking is changing, quite dramatically in some cases. Significant efforts are being made to 'empower' people, to give them responsibility, discretion, freedom and the opportunity to make decisions. The new approach has resulted in increased productivity, quality and a caring for work, services and products that was never possible under the old modes of thinking.

For these changes to take place, a whole new management philosophy has had to develop so that work is organized in a different way. Managers themselves have had to change their behaviour and create the climate of freedom in which people can operate, grow and develop both their jobs and themselves.

Method

1. Explain the purpose of the exercise. Distribute Handout 6.1 to each participant and explain that it is aimed at measuring the working climate in their section or department as they perceive it. This is directly related to the managerial style and philosophy adopted.

2. Point out that the survey examines fifteen aspects of the working climate. Participants should consider each aspect and tick the point on the scale that applies. Appropriate comments should also be added.

3. On completion of the survey managers should be formed into groups of about six participants. If there are managers present from the same department or section, then they should be grouped together as their collective analyses will benefit them.

A coordinator is appointed for each group. They have to collate each participant's score on Handout 6.2. This handout, showing the scores of the group, is then copied on to flipchart paper and presented for discussion. The score patterns are analysed by the group.

4. As a review of each of the fifteen sections takes place, an action plan should be developed on Handout 6.3 which shows:

    (a)   the action that the individual manager will take;
    (b)   the factors that need to be brought to the attention of more senior management.

5. Debrief the activity by asking selected participants to discuss their action plans and encourage a discussion. Allow managers to elaborate on how they have developed conducive working climates in the past and the benefits gained. Discuss as necessary any of the points made in the Trainer Guidance section.

Timing

1. Introducing the exercises and Handout 6.1 takes ten minutes.

2. Completing Handout 6.1 takes forty minutes.

3. Analysing and discussing results takes sixty minutes.

4. Completing Handout 6.3 takes sixty minutes.

5. Debriefing takes fifteen minutes.

Average total time: three hours five minutes.

Materials required

1. Sufficient copies of Handouts 6.1, 6.2 and 6.3.

2. Flipchart and marker pens.

Working climate survey

Think of the section or department in which you work and consider the climate and conditions that exist. Complete the attached questionnaire by taking one area at a time, reading the two statements at either end of the scale and placing a tick (✓) where you perceive your section or department to be. Add brief comments to support your position. When completing the survey, try to think generally about your situation rather than let one particular incident or circumstance cloud your judgement.

PEOPLE

People are seen and treated as secondary to other factors   1 2 3 4 5 6 7   People are seen and treated as the principal asset.

Brief comments

STANDARDS

We have low standards and are generally lax.   1 2 3 4 5 6 7   We aim for and achieve excellence in all that we do.

Brief comments

CONTRIBUTION

People are seen as having little to offer and contribute.   1 2 3 4 5 6 7   At all times, people are encouraged to contribute and their efforts are greatly valued.

Brief comments

49

LOYALTY AND COMMITMENT

Loyalty and commitment are minimal and are actively discouraged.

1 2 3 4 5 6 7

Loyalty and commitment are very high and are encouraged at all times.

Brief comments

INFORMATION

People are kept in the dark and know little about what is going on.

1 2 3 4 5 6 7

Information is readily shared and everybody knows what is happening.

Brief comments

JOBS

Jobs are so designed and arranged that they are generally unsatisfactory and unenjoyable.

1 2 3 4 5 6 7

Great satisfaction and enjoyment are built into all jobs.

Brief comments

PERSONAL AND TEAM DEVELOPMENT

There is little personal or team development using formalized techniques.

1 2 3 4 5 6 7

Personal and team development is very advanced using formalized techniques.

Brief comments

Reproduced from *Activities for Public Sector Training: Achieving Change and Strengthening Teamwork,*
Gower Publishing Ltd.

JOB DEVELOPMENT

There is little or no job development or reorganization taking place.

1 2 3 4 5 6 7

Continual job development and reorganization are our normal methods of operating.

Brief comments

MANAGEMENT CONTROL

Management has the place in a strait-jacket and it is impossible to do anything without their say-so.

1 2 3 4 5 6 7

There is minimal management control apart from that guaranteeing a safe and economic operation.

Brief comments

ESTEEM AND TRUST

Esteem and trust are very low or non-existent in members.

1 2 3 4 5 6 7

Esteem and trust are very high in all members.

Brief comments

TEAMWORK AND LOYALTY

Loyalty, teamwork and cohesiveness are almost non-existent among members.

1 2 3 4 5 6 7

Strong loyalty, cohesiveness and teamwork are shared by all members.

Brief comments

QUALITY AND VALUE

Our customers and consumers receive products that are poor both in value and quality.

1 2 3 4 5 6 7

We provide our customers and consumers with products of excellent value and quality

Brief comments

NEEDS, AMBITIONS AND ASPIRATIONS

No account is taken of members' needs, ambitions and aspirations.

1 2 3 4 5 6 7

Every opportunity is given for members to satisfy their needs, ambitions and aspirations.

Brief comments

SELF-SUFFICIENCY

Management policy and action are repressive and restrictive, allowing little individual or team self-sufficiency.

1 2 3 4 5 6 7

All teams and individuals are allowed to operate with self-sufficiency within safety and commercial constraints.

Brief comments

DEVOLUTION

Little authority or responsibility is passed down to the teams from management.

1 2 3 4 5 6 7

At all times, maximum authority and responsibility is given to the team.

Brief comments

Working climate survey

Group analysis

Collate each participant's score on this profile, so that the overall pattern of the group can be seen.

	1	2	3	4	5	6	7
People							
Standards							
Contribution							
Loyalty and commitment							
Information							
Jobs							
Personal and team development							
Job development							
Management control							
Esteem and trust							
Teamwork and loyalty							
Quality and value							
Needs, ambitions and aspirations							
Self-sufficiency							
Devolution							

Working climate survey

Action plan

For each of the items on the profile describe actions that you feel should be taken to bring about an improvement. Categorize the actions into those that *you* can take and those that should be taken by more senior management.

1. People
2. Standards
3. Contribution
4. Loyalty and commitment

5. Information

6. Jobs

7. Personal and team development

8. Job development

9. Management control

10. Esteem and trust

11.	Teamwork and loyalty
12.	Quality and value
13.	Needs, ambitions and aspirations
14.	Self-sufficiency
15.	Devolution

7

Operation improvement

Description

This activity helps to raise participants' awareness of quality issues through conducting a quality and service survey using their own experience as 'customers'.

Situations

The activity can be used alone or as part of a quality/customer care programme. It is suitable for managers, supervisors or any person involved in service provision.

The activity is designed to be run in the venue where you are holding your training event – ideally a training centre or conference facility where some degree of service is provided. If the training venue is not suitable for this exercise you could modify the activity to focus on an internal service which is regularly used by all participants, such as canteen or office services etc.

Objectives

- To alert participants to quality, standards and improvement.

- To give practice in identifying and planning improvement.

Trainer guidance

Quality, standards and service improvement are now very important issues for public sector organizations and are a central factor in management philosophy and business planning. The introduction of competitive working practices and citizen's charter initiatives have led to significant rethinking of public sector staff attitudes and to the development of numerous quality programmes.

This exercise helps to raise participants' awareness of quality issues by conducting a quality and service survey of the establishment as a means of raising each individual's understanding of quality.

The first part of the exercise is done individually and then carried out in groups of about six people.

Method

1. Explain the purpose of the exercise, stressing the importance of quality and service to the survival and success of any organization.

2. Distribute a copy of Handout 7.1 to each participant and explain the four parts of the exercise. Form groups of about six people and distribute copies of Handouts 7.2, 7.3 and 7.4 to each participant. Assist them through the four stages as necessary, especially in writing the improvement plan and planning the presentation.

3. At the presentation, comment on the quality of the presentations and the commercial feasibility of the plans. If you think it appropriate, the training centre managers can be invited to the presentations so that they receive feedback on the service offered and also assist participants in their learning.

4. Review the exercise with the participants and broaden it out to a general discussion on quality. Use the headings on Handout 7.5 and emphasize the points highlighted in the Trainer Guidance section.

5. Ensure that participants understand that in the longer term, poor quality can be very costly.

6. Stress the importance of each individual in bringing about improvements in quality.

Timing

1. Explaining the importance of quality and service takes ten minutes.

2. The individual task takes thirty minutes.

3. The group task takes thirty minutes.

4. The improvement plan takes thirty minutes.

5. The plan presentation takes thirty minutes.

6. Presentations from each group take twenty minutes.

7. Review and debriefing take twenty minutes.

The exercise takes between two hours fifty minutes and three hours thirty minutes, depending on the number of groups.

Materials required

1. Sufficient copies of Handouts 7.1, 7.2, 7.3 and 7.4.

2. Copy of Handout 7.5 for the trainer.

3. Flipchart, paper and marker pens.

4. A training centre or hotel.

Operation improvement: instructions

This exercise is in four parts:

1. **Individual task**

   In this first task, you are to think about and reflect upon your experience of the training centre since you came here. How have you felt about the initial reception, the facilities, decor, service and staff, and anything else that may be improved? Try to think about the good and not so good things. List on Handout 7.2 the six most important areas requiring attention. If necessary, walk round the centre to refresh your memory of the main features. You have thirty minutes to complete this task.

2. **Group task**

   In your groups discuss your individual lists and agree a group list of the six most important features requiring attention. It is likely that you will have some common features and some that are individual to each person. By discussion, debate and consensus, agree one list to which you can all subscribe. Record this on Handout 7.3. You have thirty minutes to complete this task.

3. **Improvement plan**

   Still working in your groups draw up an improvement plan using Handout 7.4. You will have to think about the actions required to put into effect your recommendations. It now becomes a management document that could be discussed by the management of the training centre. Any of the actions that you recommend have to be assessed for their commercial feasibility. For example you may recommend structural changes to the building but this could be commercially impossible as the organization may not have the capital to carry them out. On the other hand, something like the retraining of reception staff could have a marked effect and would cost relatively little. You have thirty minutes to complete this task.

4. **Presentations**

   Each group should now plan and deliver a presentation of their improvement plan to the other groups in plenary session. It should be delivered in a professional manner using an overhead projector or flip-chart. The group should organize itself and decide how the presentation will be conducted and who will speak. This may be one or several speakers. Planning the presentation should take thirty minutes and the presentation itself should last for twenty minutes.

Operation improvement: individual task

Possible improvement areas

List the six in order of importance with 1 the most important, and so on.

1.

2.

3.

4.

5.

6.

Operation improvement: group task

Improvement areas

List the six in order of importance that all the group agree on, with 1 the most important and so on.

1.

2.

3.

4.

5.

6.

Operation improvement: improvement plan

Improvement area	Importance* 1:2:3	Action required	Time to complete	Cost

Importance*

1. Very important – will have a big effect on the centre.
2. Moderately important – will have a reasonable effect on the centre.
3. Slightly important – will have a significant but small effect on the centre.

69

Operation improvement: review sheet

The objective of this review is to consolidate and expand on the participants' views of what quality is and its importance to organizations. To this end, discussions should be held on the following points:

- How is quality defined?

- What are the components of a quality product or service?

- Do all people perceive quality in the same way? If not, what are the reasons for the difference?

- Do high quality products and services entail high investment in resources?

- What examples can participants think of where the cost of high quality has been minimal?

- What must an organization do to produce high quality goods and services?

- How important is each individual employee in obtaining and sustaining high quality?

- What are the three fundamental factors that give rise to high quality?

8

Making changes

Description

This activity is a role play exercise involving a staff meeting where change is discussed.

Situations

The activity is most useful for managers and supervisors who are required to implement change within their staff team. It can be used in a programme on managing change or as part of a more general management/supervisory skills course. It can also be used with an existing staff team as a participative case study.

A minimum of three people is needed to run the role play but it will be most effective with six to eight participants. For groups of more than eight, two or more role plays can be run simultaneously.

Objectives

- To enable managers to explore ways of involving staff in decision making and implementing change.

- To enable managers and supervisors to explore ways of making change work with a staff team.

Trainer guidance

This is a very true-to-life role play: lack of participation in staff meetings or 'lukewarm' or negative attitudes to change are a problem many managers have to work with. The realism can be increased by asking those playing managers to use issues that are real to them – as long as these are not too complex for other participants to work with in the time available.

Some key points to develop from the activity are:

1. To make changes, you have to be prepared to take risks, and not resort to the normal fall-back position.

2. Staff need to feel safe and valued to be able to start to accept changes.

3. It takes a while to convince others that you mean it if you are trying to do things differently, and they will try to push you back into old patterns.

Method

1. Describe the situation to the whole group.

2. Ask for volunteers to be the manager in the situation. The number of managers needed depends on the size of the group you are working with and the number of role plays you are running.

3. Give the managers their brief and divide the rest of the participants into two groups. Give one of the groups Staff Brief 1 and the other group Staff Brief 2. NB: There are two different briefs for staff to encourage representation of two different perspectives on change – one sceptical yet interested if it proves to be a genuine change, the other resistant because comfortable with the 'way things are'.

4. Allow some time for reading the briefs and preparation.

5. Set up the role play with clear meeting space for the teams. Ensure that each role play includes both Staff Briefs.

6. Allow forty-five minutes to run the role play.

7. Ask each team to discuss the role play among themselves, using the following structured questions which you can put up on a flipchart:

    ● What were the different reactions which you experienced?
    ● What made the manager's declared intention convincing?
    ● What made you feel that it was worthwhile contributing?
    ● What would you want to happen next?

    Ask them to record summaries of their responses on a flipchart.

8. As a whole group, discuss the implications of instigating changes with your own staff teams.

Timing

1. Introduction and setting up the role play takes ten minutes.

2. Preparation time takes twenty minutes.

3. Running the role play takes forty-five minutes.

4. Team and full group discussion takes half an hour to forty minutes.

Average total time: one hour forty-five minutes to two hours.

Materials required

1. Sufficient copies of Handouts 8.1, 8.2 and 8.3.

2. Flipchart, paper and pens.

3. Suitable working space for each role play group.

Manager's brief

You have instigated a weekly staff meeting because you want to involve your team more fully in decision making and in the implementation of new working practices. This came about as a result of a management team away-day where you became convinced that more staff involvement and participation would make a positive difference to morale and motivation.

Your staff team are pleasant and helpful and agree with your points. They also say that they appreciate the idea of weekly meetings and your intention to involve them in decision making. However they don't suggest any items for the agenda. When you ask if anyone does or does not want to be involved in a project they say, 'I don't mind', and you find in the end that you tell them what to do.

You wanted to change the way the section operated but they seem to prefer you to have the responsibility for decisions and ideas. You find this frustrating because you believe that a different approach would be good for service delivery and for the staff and you don't understand why they are not reacting as you expected.

You have decided to try a different approach to the weekly meeting this time. You are going to cancel the official meeting and ask if they would help you to find an approach to a problem or a project you want to tackle – where you genuinely have not yet decided how to proceed.

Possible issues might be a difficult client or service user, how to reorganize a work area, writing a mission statement etc. It is useful to take something which is real for you, if it exists, and use the opportunity to learn from other people's ideas.

Staff brief 1

You have been with this organization and your manager for a while, and you're used to the way the place runs. It suits you: you're told what to do, but the manager is fair, considerate and a good manager overall.

Recently all senior managers attended an away-day on implementing change in the organization. They came back with many ideas and your manager intends to have weekly meetings and involve the team more in the running of the section. This has happened before – when your manager has been on a course and decides to make changes as a result. You know that after the initial enthusiasm, things soon slip back to normal.

You've been going to the weekly meetings and played along with this new idea but, as you feared, nothing is really changing. You expect that the meetings will stop soon and the idea forgotten.

You do sometimes think of something that you would like to suggest and you would quite enjoy taking more responsibility but you don't feel your manager is serious about this.

Staff brief 2

You have been with this organization and your manager for a while, and you're used to the way the place runs. It suits you: you're told what to do, but the manager is fair, considerate and a good manager overall.

Recently all senior managers attended an away-day on implementing change in the organization. They came back with many ideas and your manager intends to have weekly meetings and involve the team more in the running of the section. This has happened before – when your manager has been on a course and decides to make changes as a result. You know that after the initial enthusiasm, things soon slip back to normal. However you're a bit worried this time. Your manager seems to be more keen than usual on this particular idea and is not so willing to let go of it.

However, s/he is still arranging everything beforehand and when no one else makes any suggestions at the meetings, then s/he does so as usual. So you think that this phase will probably pass.

9

Opting for green

Description

This is a group activity which brings topical, service and environmental issues into a managerial development forum.

Situations

The activity can be part of a training course on planning, team building, creativity and communication. It contains a competitive element which adds the dimension of high energy and motivation levels.

Objectives

- To show the need for effective communication in any team activity.

- To reinforce the need to plan any activity if resources are to be used to their maximum effect.

Trainer guidance

This is a very topical activity in that it brings together groups of participants to examine creatively ways of helping their services 'opt for green'. That is, to discuss and recommend aspects of the service which would benefit from a new, 'environmental green' approach.

The debrief should centre on participants' feelings regarding the energy levels in the team, why they were so committed, their own motivation levels etc. These can then be related to how they can bring these feelings into their jobs.

Method

1. Divide the participants into groups of four.

2. Give out the Participant's Brief (Handout 9.1) and go through the planning phase.

3. Explain the objectives of the exercise, stressing the fact that the recommendations they come up with must be realistic and achievable.

4. After the planning phase, reconvene the groups for their presentations and voting by the trainer. (The trainer can give a casting vote if necessary or develop a different scoring method as required.)

5. Debrief the exercise.

Timing

1. The planning phase should take one hour.

2. The presentation phase should take half an hour, depending on the number of groups.

3. The debriefing of the activity should take half an hour.

Materials required

1. Separate areas for teams to plan and prepare.

2. Sufficient copies of the Participant's Brief (Handout 9.1).

3. Flipchart and marker pens.

Participants' brief

Your organization has decided to 'opt for green'. The environmental issues affecting the planet at the present time have reached the consciences of your members/directors. They are now looking to you and your colleagues as a 'green think tank' to come up with three brilliant, creative, cost-saving ideas for the organization to adopt. They have also asked other groups for the same information. Only one group can have its ideas put forward at the next major decision-making meeting. You and your team must try to ensure those views are yours by producing quality ideas.

Your three recommended ideas must be realistic and achievable for the organization.

You have sixty minutes to plan your ten minute presentation to the ideas coordinator (the course tutor!) and your other 'green' competitors.

Every member of the team must have a part to play in the presentation in order to show your team's total belief in your ideas.

10

Shifting our attitudes to service

Description

A challenging activity which takes a look at why customer service goes wrong and examines the impact of social attitudes together with 'management controllable' failings. The activity also prompts participants to consider how they could influence supplier service by means of their own behaviour.

Situations

Suitable for all levels of employee but particularly management and supervisory staff.

Objectives

- To discuss why customer service goes wrong.
- To identify customer service failings within participants' organizations.
- To consider ways of reducing these failings.
- To identify ways in which participants can influence supplier service.

Trainer guidance

Attitudes to customer service are affected by the social attitudes of the individual, the group and also by the degree of management commitment to service. This activity examines two areas: management failings and social attitudes.

Management failings cover such issues as poor selection of employees, lack of good-quality training, low morale, poor job satisfaction, inadequate supervision and weak career structures. Also covered are industrial relations problems, operational inefficiencies and conflict due to the nature of the job.

Social attitudes stem from factors such as background, family influence, circle of friends, media influence and experiences to date. They are manifested in behaviours towards other people, for example political and discriminatory stances, exploitation of less powerful groups etc.

Management failings and social attitude problems, with regard to customer service, will manifest themselves in the form of things going wrong at the point of customer contact, such as face-to-face communication, the ability to listen and empathize, the manner and style of letter writing, telephone techniques and the handling of complaints.

Understanding, accepting and admitting the underlying reasons for customer service failures is half the battle. Shifting attitudes, many of which are deeply ingrained, is not easy. This requires bold and active commitment from the top and will only be maintained through constant vigilance.

Within the framework of this activity, a primary role as trainer is to facilitate discussion of these important issues. The trainer should also move participants forward towards suggesting ways in which attitudes can be changed and how they, as individuals, can influence the service given. It is important to ensure that the focus is on issues participants can change and influence, rather that on political decisions or resource issues over which they have no control.

Method

1. After a brief introduction, divide participants into groups of four or five and distribute a copy of Handout 10.1 to each participant. Ask groups to address each question and prepare to report their finding to the main group.

2. In the main group, arrange presentations and record key points on a flipchart. Discuss and allow sufficient time for questions.

3. Re-form participants into their groups and ask them to consider the following questions, which can be written up on a flipchart, again, preparing themselves to report to the main group:

    *   How would you, as managers, encourage positive attitudes towards providing customer service in your department? Specifically, what would you do?
    *   How could you, as individuals, influence the service that you get from other parts of the organization or from external suppliers? Specifically, what could you do?

4. In the main group, ask groups to report their answers. Make sure that a full discussion on common ground and differences takes place, and also ask participants to record points of agreement.

5. Allow time for participants to decide and write down four statements of what they intend to do differently as providers of service and as receivers of service (two statements for each role). Ask participants to announce their intentions publicly. Finally, review the learning from the activity.

Timing

1. Completing Handout 10.1 takes thirty to forty-five minutes.

2. Presentations and discussion takes forty-five to fifty minutes.

3. Preparing answers to questions takes thirty to forty minutes.

4. Feedback, discussion and recording points takes forty-five to fifty minutes.

5. Individual statements and review takes thirty minutes.

Average total time: half a day, including breaks.

Materials required

1. Sufficient copies of Handout 10.1.

2. Sufficient space for participants to work undisturbed.

3. Flipchart, paper and pens.

Attitudes to service

A complaint often heard is that public sector organizations fail to provide the service that customers are entitled to. The aim of this exercise is to discuss:

(a) exactly *what* goes wrong; and

(b) *why* it goes wrong.

You should investigate these two fundamental questions by discussing the following. Please record your group's responses on to a flipchart for subsequent presentation and discussion in the main group.

1. When customer service fails, what specifically goes wrong? (Brainstorm if necessary.)

2. Focus on failures that generally stem from management control or from social attitude problems. Categorize these issues under two headings:

Management failings   **Social attitude problems**

3. Which deep seated social attitudes affect your organization?

4. Which of these affect face-to-face service, and how?

5. What are the top five causes of less than perfect service in your organization?

Part II
Change management skills

11

Building my consultancy style

Description

This activity looks at consultancy in its widest sense, including situations where people are helped to solve problems, seek improvements or achieve change.

Participants examine the consultant role and identify situations in which they act as consultant. They also design a model of effective consulting against which they contrast their own style and performance to form conclusions about areas for improvement.

Situations

Suitable for anyone who wishes to examine and explore their effectiveness in the role of consultant – within or outside their organization.

Objectives

- To concentrate on situations in which participants take on the role of consultant.
- To sharpen their understanding of an effective consulting process.
- To draw conclusions about their own performance in a recent consultancy role and identify areas for improvement and further development.
- To identify and commit themselves to some new behaviours to be used in future consulting roles.

Trainer guidance

The word 'consultant' conjures up many different perceptions: some people view consultancy as 'not for them'; others see the value in using an impartial third party to assist them in clarifying their situation and moving forward. In this activity, whilst the usual terms of 'consultant' and 'client' are used, consultancy style is addressed in its widest sense.

You may be working with people who have explicit consultant roles, with the need to prepare formal proposals, detailed terms of reference, well defined evaluation criteria and established service-level agreements. On the other hand, your group may include people who, from time to time, work with others in a 'helping' capacity, asking questions, listening, focusing and generally enabling their 'clients' to take decisions and move on.

One of your core roles in this activity is to enable participants to arrive at a model of the consulting process which they feel comfortable with. Another is to encourage participants to accept the value of using such a process, whether formally or informally, when adopting the role of consultant.

Another important point is to recognize the opportunities presented to you, as trainer, for modelling the consultancy process during the activity. You will be able to demonstrate many of the consultancy skills as you enable participants (your 'clients') to work through the activity. Participants' understanding and learning can be enhanced by drawing attention to this and by encouraging them to observe, question and discuss specific examples as the activity progresses.

Method

1. Give a brief introduction, followed by a discussion on the terms 'consultant' and 'consultancy' in order to bring out the depth and breadth of perceptions. Brainstorming can be used, or some type of memory or brain pattern technique which helps participants to illustrate their thoughts, to help the flow of ideas. Recording of key words and statements will help the process. If the distinction does not naturally emerge then encourage discussion on 'internal' and 'external' consultant: this should enable participants to accept that they will all, at some time, be acting as 'internal' consultant to someone.

2. Divide participants into pairs, distribute Handout 11.1, and allow forty-five minutes to complete the tasks.

3. Bring participants together and share the results obtained by the pairs. Encourage discussion, questions and free flow of information. Produce a consolidated list of the range of consultant roles.

4. Divide participants into groups of four or five and brief them for the following task:

Produce a visual aid showing the 'consultancy process': this should highlight the various stages. For each stage, show what needs to happen together with the skills and competences required by the consultant for effective performance.

You may wish to distribute Handout 11.2 to groups to use to help in designing their 'model process'.

5. In a plenary session invite groups to present their 'model processes': encourage questions and full discussion both on the 'processes' and the actions and consultant competence elements.
    After the presentations, allow time for participants to modify their 'models' if they feel this to be necessary. At the end of this step ensure participants are in possession of a 'model consultancy process' which they believe is suited to them.

6. Divide participants into groups of two or three, distribute Handout 11.3, and allow approximately one hour to complete the tasks.

7. Bring participants together and ask them to explain publicly their intentions for change. Draw attention to the following questions:

    ●   What further training do I feel in need of?
        (It may be possible to contract for this during the session.)
    ●   Who can assist and support me with my plan?
        (There may be people in the group who can offer help.)
    ●   What opportunities do I recognize for practising my consultancy approach further?

Finally, ask participants to comment on examples of consultancy practice which they have witnessed during the activity and review the learning which they believe they have gained during the process.

Timing

1. Introduction and discussion takes twenty minutes.

2. Completing Handout 11.1 takes forty-five minutes.

3. Sharing and producing a consolidated list takes forty to fifty minutes.

4. Group task takes sixty to eighty minutes.

5. Presentation and modification of models takes forty-five to sixty minutes.

6. Completing Handout 11.3 takes fifty to sixty minutes.

7. Publicizing intentions for change and contracting and learning review takes one hour thirty minutes to two hours.

Average total time: one day.

Materials required

1. Sufficient copies of Handouts 11.1, 11.2 and 11.3.
2. Sufficient space for participants to work undisturbed.
3. Paper, pens, flipcharts, OHP and acetates.

Identifying different consultancy roles

Individually, and then with your partner, carry out the following tasks in the time allowed:

1. Individually, think through and record the types of situations in which you take on the role of consultant. Record also the types of 'client'.

2. Working with your partner, help each other to define the different types of consultant role for each situation identified. This should highlight a range of roles demonstrating, for example, the varying degrees of influence held by consultant and client.

3. Jointly produce a flipchart, or other visual aid, showing the range of consultant roles you have identified. Rank them in some order of your own choosing; for example, increasing influence of consultant, increasing expectation of client, etc. For each role give a brief example of one of your own experiences.

Framework for thinking about the consultancy process

Before the consultancy

- Background research
- Knowledge of client and client's situation
- Stocktake of own skills and resources
- Outline plan for the consultancy

Start of the consultancy

- Initial contract (how, when and who with)
- Building rapport and trust
- Confirming the need for consultancy

During the consultancy

- Agreeing the focus of the work
- The basis of the 'contract'
- Clarifying roles and expectations of both parties
- Desired outcomes from the work
- The diagnosis, including methods
- Managing the work

Towards the end of the consultancy

- Reporting back to the client
- Gaining the client's commitment to action
- Evaluating the work done
- Consultant's withdrawal and agreeing next steps

After the consultancy

- Future relationship
- Follow-up activities

Assessing individual performance and deciding areas for change

Individually and then in groups of two or three, carry out the following tasks in the time allowed.

1. Individually, decide on a recent experience, where you took on the role of consultant. Using the 'model consultancy process' think carefully about your performance at each stage. Make notes showing where you performed well and not so well; briefly jot down your ideas on how you might have behaved differently.

2. Share with your partner(s) your recent consultancy experience and encourage each other to describe the aspects which were performed well. Listen very carefully to each other and be prepared to ask questions.

3. Now help each other to describe those aspects which could have been more effective. Encourage each other to concentrate on the skills which require developing and/or the new behaviours which you are prepared to try in the future. Write down key thoughts on how these changes can be achieved.

12

Triggering my ability to influence others

Lord, grant me the courage to change those things that need to be changed, the strength to endure those things that cannot be changed and the wisdom to know the difference.
(Prayer attributed to St Francis)

Description

This activity considers the skills, qualities and abilities that are needed to influence others, and explores ways in which these can be 'triggered' in ourselves in order to influence others more effectively.

Situations

This activity can be used by anyone who needs to influence others more effectively, for example:

- senior managers involved in changing the culture of the organization;

- managers trying to introduce different ways of working;

- individuals hoping to influence policies and practices.

Objectives

- To identify some of the skills and qualities needed to influence others.

- To recognize the negative and positive aspects of influence.

- To develop strategies for acquiring and/or improving the skills/qualities needed for effectively influencing others.

Trainer guidance

You will need to be aware of the negative and positive aspects of influencing and be able to help people explore these issues in a safe, realistic way. If not handled well, this activity could be seen to be encouraging people to manipulate others.

Method

1. Ask the participants to think about someone they feel has greatly influenced them or others in a favourable or unfavourable way. This could be a famous person – for example Mother Theresa, Richard Branson, or someone close to them – for example a partner, parent or friend. Then ask participants to brainstorm the qualities, skills and behaviours demonstrated by people who influenced them favourably, followed by the same exercise for those who influenced them un-favourably. For example:

    *   Favourable: example, encouragement, etc.
    *   Unfavourable: fear, power, etc.

    Lead a discussion on the differences and similarities displayed by both groups and what this tells us about influence.

2. Divide participants into small groups and ask them individually to complete Handout 12.1. Instruct them to discuss and share areas/ situations when they succeeded in influencing and how it felt. Also discuss and share areas/situations when they failed to influence and how that felt. Record on a flipchart common feelings in both successful and failed influencing situations.

    Bring participants together and ask each group to report back on their discussions, using their flipcharts. Follow this with a discussion on common areas and sharing of key learning gained from this exercise.

3. Produce a checklist of Dos and Don'ts of influencing. You may wish to have the list reproduced as a Handout for the participants.

Timing

1. Identifying influential people, brainstorming and discussion takes thirty to forty-five minutes.

2. Completing Handout 12.1 and identifying key learning takes forty to sixty minutes.

3. Producing checklist takes ten to fifteen minutes.

Average total time: one hour forty minutes.

Materials required

1. Sufficient copies of Handout 12.1.
2. Flipcharts and pens.
3. Sufficient rooms for groups to work in undisturbed.

My spheres of influence matrix

	My family/friends (the people around me)	My work colleagues (the people where I work)	Others (people in the world around me)
When I influence or have influenced			
How I influence or have influenced			
Why I influence or have influenced			
Where I influence or have influenced			

13

First-class travel

Description

This activity is a case study which can be used in negotiation training. The negotiation can be conducted on a one-to-one basis or in small teams, such as negotiation between the administrative assistant and the owner of a coach firm.

Situations

As the activity is a negotiation exercise and requires participants to use a variety of negotiating skills, it can be used on almost any negotiation training event. It is especially useful for staff who are involved in selling or buying services. As questioning, listening and communication skills are involved, this activity can also be used in interpersonal skills training or in change management where communication and aspects of negotiation are important.

Objectives

- To practise negotiating on a one-to-one basis.

- To identify personal negotiating strengths and weaknesses.

- To identify the needs of both purchasers and providers in negotiations and thereby broaden understanding of the negotiation process.

Trainer guidance

As the activity includes detailed briefs there are a few problems for the trainer. Some participants may need help to think themselves into the roles or to expand the brief as they feel necessary.

Method

One trainer would normally be able to organize a group of up to eight participants in this activity, for instance by setting up three groups of one-to-one negotiations. The two remaining members could be nominated to act as observers and help the trainer with feedback. An alternative is to use two groups of two-to-two, in which the administrative assistant could be joined by a finance assistant and the coach firm owner by a booking clerk.

1. Equip each room with a table and chairs for negotiators and any observers. If possible record the negotiation using closed circuit television as this will enhance the debriefing session.

2. Allocate roles to participants and distribute the briefs, Handouts 13.2 and 13.3. Brief the observers and agree the extent and specific areas they should note. Request the participants to extract the relevant information from the briefs and prepare their negotiating stance.

3. After checking that participants are fully prepared, begin the negotiations. Observe each discussion, making notes of any significant stages to use in later analysis.

4. Following the negotiations invite all participants to reassemble. Ask each group to confirm the 'deal' that has been agreed and record it on a flipchart.
   Ask each group to comment on their 'satisfaction' level prior to discussing their performance with the observers.

Timing

1. The introduction to the activity and allocating roles and rooms takes ten minutes.

2. Preparation will take twenty minutes.

3. The negotiations will take up to thirty minutes to conclude.

4. At least forty-five minutes will be needed to discuss the negotiations and agree good practice (longer if video is used).

The total average time taken: one and three quarters to two hours.

Materials required

1. Sufficient copies of Handout 13.1 for trainers and observers.
2. Sufficient copies of Handouts 13.2 and 13.3 for those taking roles.
3. Sufficient quiet space for the negotiations to take place.
4. A calculator for each group.

Trainer's brief

This brief provides an overview of the negotiation and the key elements from both sides.

Administrative assistant

The administrative assistant's task is to organize a coach trip to Blackpool for 175 people. These are users of social services day care and residential units, carers and staff. The service users are mainly elderly people or those with learning difficulties. All are physically and mentally able to make the trip without distress and to enjoy the occasion.

The journey to Blackpool takes three hours and the plan is to set off at 10am and leave Blackpool at 8pm.

A stop for lunch can be made on the way, although the service users prefer to spend as much time as possible in Blackpool.

A budget of £1400 is available.

The best quotation obtained so far is five forty-seater standard coaches at £135 each. Buffet lunch will be provided at a hotel on the way at £4.30 per head.

The trip is to be on a Tuesday.

Coach firm

The coach firm has eleven coaches as follows:

- Six luxury forty-seater coaches, including toilet and buffet – normal charge for this journey, £170 per coach.

- Three standard forty-seater coaches with no on-board facilities – normal charge for this journey, £125 per coach.

- Two minibus twenty-seater coaches – normal charge for this journey, £80 per minibus.

A buffet lunch can be served on the luxury coaches at £3.25 per passenger.

A charge of £10 per coach hour (or part thereof) is made for coaches returning to the depot after 10pm. Half of this is given to the driver.

One of the standard coaches is already booked for the date given. The busiest time for the coaches are Thursday to Sunday.

At the above prices, the firm makes a profit of 30 per cent.

Administrative assistant's brief

You are an administrative assistant in a social services section. You have been asked by the director of social services to organize a coach trip to Blackpool for 175 people. These are users of social services day care and residential units, carers and staff. The service users are mainly elderly people or those with learning difficulties. All are physically and mentally able to make the trip without distress and to enjoy the occasion.

The following facts pertain:

1. You have a budget of £1400 to cover transport and lunch. Tea and an evening meal will be provided free in Blackpool. All other expenses will be paid for by the individuals concerned or from petty cash.

2. The outing should be on a Tuesday in October.

3. You would like to set off at 10am and leave Blackpool at 8pm.

4. The service users wish to spend as much time as possible in Blackpool.

5. The best quotation you have so far received is five standard forty-seater coaches at £135 each. In addition, this firm would arrange a buffet lunch at a hotel on the way for £4.30 per head.

Your brief is to try to get the best possible deal for the service users and for the department.

Coach firm owner's brief

You are the owner of a coach firm which has been approached by a social services department to provide transport for a trip to Blackpool on a Tuesday in October.

The coach firm has eleven coaches as follows:

- Six luxury forty-seater coaches, including toilet and buffet – normal charge for this journey, £170 per coach.

- Three standard forty-seater coaches with no on-board facilities – normal charge for this journey £125 per coach.

- Two minibus twenty-seater coaches – normal charge for this journey, £80 per minibus.

A buffet lunch can be served on the luxury coaches at £3.25 per passenger.

A charge of £10 per coach hour (or part thereof) is made for coaches returning to the depot after 10pm. Half of this is given to the driver.

One of the standard coaches is already booked for the date given. The busiest times for the coaches are Thursday to Sunday.

At the above prices, the firm makes a profit of 30 per cent.

You are keen to secure this contract and to make a deal but also to protect your profit margin.

14

Excuses, excuses

Description

In this activity participants role play a manager leading a team meeting in which performance problems are discussed.

Situations

This activity is useful in training programmes dealing with communication skills, staff management, performance problems and running team meetings.

The role play can be run in groups of four, five or six, with three or four people playing roles and one or two observing. This can be modified to suit the needs of any particular group.

Objectives

- To provide an opportunity for managers to consider ways in which they communicate priorities to their teams.

- To provide an opportunity to practise effective communication in addressing performance problems.

Trainer guidance

Role play activities provide excellent opportunities for learning and can be thought-provoking and enlightening. However they often meet with resistance from participants and you may need to offer support and assistance to encourage participants to take part. It is useful to emphasize the valuable learning that can be gained and the 'safety' of trying out this sort of activity in a training environment.

There is a strong element of conflict in this role play which, combined with the exposure of the manager in the suggested method, may be threatening. If you feel this would be unproductive, it is better to run the role play in small groups, each with an observer.

In the feedback session, ensure that feedback is given in a constructive manner, rather than being over-critical.

Learning points you may wish to emphasize are:

1. The manager needs to convince the team that it is for their benefit that s/he is giving them extra tasks.

2. They need to be able to see that delegating tasks is not merely an avoidance of work on the part of the manager.

3. The manager needs to stay aware of what the team already has to do, and take that into account.

Method

1. Briefly describe the content of the role play and establish that it is a regular team meeting.

2. Ask for a minimum of four volunteers, three to form the team and one to be the manager. Give these people copies of the briefs (Handouts 14.1 and 14.2) and ask them to read them through and prepare themselves.

3. Ask the rest of the group to act as observers. Give them copies of Handouts 14.1 and 14.2. Half of the observing group are to observe the team and how they begin to be influenced into observing the manager's viewpoint. The other half are to observe the manager and the strategies used to begin to change the position of the team.

4. Run the role play.

5. Ask the manager and team members to discuss their perceptions of the role play first, focusing on effective communication/influencing strategies or factors which prevented effective communication.

    Ask the observers to report their observations in turn, recording and discussing their points as they go along.

    Ask the manager to add anything else s/he can now think of that would have made a difference.

6. Divide the whole group into fours and ask them to list points to remember when communicating priorities to the team.

7. Take feedback from the whole group.

Timing

1. Introducing the exercise, setting up roles and preparation takes twenty minutes.

2. The role play takes about thirty-five minutes.

3. Discussion and stages 6 and 7 take forty-five minutes.

Total average time: one hour forty minutes.

Materials

1. Sufficient copies of Handouts 14.1 and 14.2.

2. Flipchart, paper and marker pens.

Manager's brief

You have a team meeting to lead and you need to deal with an aspect of the team's work which is causing you problems.

The three people in your team are competent and well motivated. They have specific duties and are very effective in fulfilling those responsibilities.

However they are much less effective when it comes to meeting deadlines on special projects and extra tasks you need them to carry out. These may be follow-up contacts with service users or dealing with complaints on a variety of projects which arise.

You only ask them to take on extra work which is a priority – you don't want to waste their time or yours – and you see this extra work as essential to the service and good for career development. Despite this you feel you have to constantly remind and nag them to get tasks completed and deadlines are hardly ever met. This issue is causing bad feeling in the team and you want to resolve it.

Team brief

Your team is efficient and competent and you are all on good terms. You each have set duties and responsibilities to carry out and do so well.

However your manager has a habit of dropping extra tasks on you at team meetings. These may be dealing with complaints or service user enquiries or special projects. It feels as if extra work that the manager doesn't want to do is being dumped on you and you are all beginning to resent this. You also find that you can't meet the deadlines the manager sets without affecting the priorities in your own work, so you have to try to fit these extra tasks around what you have already planned to do.

The manager becomes irritated when you don't give his/her additional tasks first priority and you suspect the issue will be raised again at the team meeting because s/he has just lost his temper with one of you about an uncompleted task.

15

Constructive confrontation

Description

This is a role play activity in which participants play out sensitive and conflict situations which have caused them problems.

Situations

The activity is useful for managers and team leaders who are required to deal with personal and performance difficulties. It is suitable for individual counselling and small group training (six to sixteen people).

Objectives

- To encourage participants to think through problem situations in terms of under-utilized strengths, abilities and resources.

- To provide an opportunity for managers to practise confronting problems without personalizing them.

Trainer guidance

You will need to take some time in the early stages of the exercise to explain the nature of constructive confrontation and to allow for some discussion of this. Encourage participants to use these points in the feedback discussion after the role play.

Method

1. Explain to participants that constructive confrontation is a set of skills in which you invite people to examine their discrepancies (that is, the human resources that are present but which are not being used, or not as fully as they might be, and perhaps those which they might be overlooking) which keep them locked into problem situations. Constructive confrontation is a means to an end. Constructive confrontation is *instrumental,* that is, constructive confrontation skills are useful to the degree that they help people develop new perspectives that enable them to define and clarify problem situations. More than this, constructive confrontation is not *destructive* confrontation. It should focus on descriptions rather than accusations.

2. One of the best ways to look at confrontation is to invite people to examine their own strengths and resources, and to discover those they are not using but which could be developed to manage a problem situation more effectively, for example:

   Problem: My influence in the company is not nearly as effective as I would like it to be.

   Description of unused strengths and resources: But I do have problem-solving skills that I don't apply to the practical problems I have described. Instead of defining goals for making myself more effective, developing the right relationships, and then seeing how many different ways I can go about achieving my goals, I just sit around and wait. I suppose I want to see if something will happen to make it happen for me. I seem to remain passive even though I have the skills to become more active and influence events.

3. Now ask participants to consider four problem situations or parts of problem situations they may have:

   - Briefly identify the problem situation.
   - Describe the problem situation or some part of it in terms of some strength, ability or resource not being used or not being used as fully as it might be.

4. Explore the responses of the participants to the problem situations, and identify unused strengths and the kind of confrontations which should be helpful.

5. Distribute copies of Handout 15.1 and set up role plays within the group. Ask the participants to take different roles – those of manager, employee and observer – each role play taking about five to ten minutes. Each member of the group should play a different role. Handout 15.1 should be completed during the role plays.

130

Ask participants to select problem situations and play out short role plays where the manager's role is to use constructive confrontation skills to tap the unused strengths in the employee. The observer should record the valuable aspects of each interaction and any additional comments that might be helpful during feedback. At the end of each role play the group as a whole should examine the effects of the confrontation skills used and whether or not these were instrumental in realizing unused strengths.

6. *Feedback/summary:* Remind participants of the role of constructive confrontation skills in developing people's resources. Emphasize that constructive confrontation is not scolding or telling the person what to do or punishing them. The main role is to help people see new ways in which they can see their situations, particularly new ways in which they can use their strengths. These may be present, but underused or not used at all. Finally, emphasize how identifying these unused strengths can be instrumental in enabling employees to achieve change and new perspectives in their lives. Record relevant items on a flipchart or overhead projector slide and invite participants to note down these significant factors.

Timing

1. Introduction and setting up the role plays takes fifteen minutes.

2. The role plays take one hour to one hour and a quarter.

3. Feedback takes about thirty minutes.

Total average time: two hours.

Materials

1. Sufficient copies of Handout 15.1.

2. Sufficient space for groups to work undisturbed.

3. Flipchart, paper and marker pens.

Statement of problem situation and unused strengths

1. Problem situation:

   Unused strengths:

2. Problem situation:

   Unused strengths:

3.   Problem situation:

Unused strengths:

4.   Problem situation:

Unused strengths:

16

Enhancing my counselling approach

Description

This activity provides an opportunity for participants to practise basic counselling skills, to discuss and receive feedback on their performance, and to form conclusions about their strengths and areas for further development.

Situations

A number of situations are suitable for this training activity, including:

1. Identifying staff who could be trained to offer a service within the organization's overall counselling provisions.

2. Enabling people who have expressed interest to experience structured counselling situations in order to decide whether they wish to proceed further in developing these skills.

3. Further development of counselling skills of people who already have some experience.

4. Managers and supervisors who need to develop some of these key skills which can be applied in their everyday work situations.

Objectives

- To practise counselling approaches with another person.

- To experience some thoughts and feelings associated with being helped by a 'counsellor'.

- To practise observation and feedback skills.

- To receive feedback on counselling performance.

- To identify personal counselling strengths together with areas for further improvement.

- To make a commitment to actions to secure improvement.

Trainer guidance

Your role is mainly facilitative, the strength of the activity being in the group sessions. Sharing in the main group provides a good platform for drawing out thoughts and feelings associated with experiencing the counselling process. As trainer, you will allow people to profit from holding their attention on the suggested points.

You may feel the need to provide some basic model(s) of the counselling process in sessions before this activity. The bibliography in Trainer's Material 16.1 offers a number of useful references for this purpose.

Before the activity, participants are asked to do some pre-course work. This is explained in Handout 16.1 which should be distributed some time before the session is due to take place.

Method

1. Before the activity, ask participants to complete the task outlined in Handout 16.1.

2. Introduce the session: the main intention of the session is to give each participant an opportunity to share his/her experience, outlined in Handout 16.1, with a 'counsellor'. In small groups each participant will play alternately the part of client, counsellor and observer.

3. Divide participants into groups of three (or four, if necessary). Distribute Handout 16.2 and ensure participants understand the three roles and the process which they are about to take part in. Stress that confidentiality will be preserved within the groups with no requirement to report back in the main group on 'specific' problems or difficulties brought by individuals. Allocate space to each group for the counselling practice sessions. Ensure privacy for each group and limit your own involvement to time management and organization.

4. Back in the main group, ask participants to express their thoughts and feelings associated with such things as:

    - being in the three roles;

- listening and being listened to;
- being helped to express something about themselves;
- someone being interested in their situation;
- being understood;
- getting stuck with helping someone else.

In this way, the participants are introduced to the early stages of the counselling process in a 'non-threatening' and safe way. The sharing in the main group is not about the 'content' of each individual 'case' but about the thoughts and feelings associated with the process.

5. Ask participants to re-form back into their groups and allow time and space for members to *help each other* to explore and identify:

    - three points they have learned which will be helpful to them in the future;

    - three strengths in their counselling approach;

    - three areas for further development together with actions for their achievement.

Timing

1. Pre-course work – completing Handout 16.1.

2. The introduction takes ten to fifteen minutes.

3. Counselling practice (three cycles – twenty minutes each including feedback) takes sixty minutes.

4. Sharing in main group takes twenty minutes.

5. Action planning takes thirty minutes.

Average total time: two hours.

Materials required

1. Sufficient copies of Handouts 16.1 and 16.2.

2. Sufficient space for groups to work undisturbed.

3. Video camera and playback facilities (optional).

Enhancing my counselling approach: pre-course work

You are invited to bring along to the session an example of a recent *work* experience which proved to be a problem/difficulty/obstacle/concern, etc.

You may wish to jot down your thoughts or notes below to help you. There will be no requirement for you to show these to other course members unless you so wish.

Counselling practice sessions

In groups of three or four, you should each share your experience, outlined in Handout 16.1, as 'client' and play the part of counsellor/observer while other members of your group share their experience. Alternate the roles so that each member plays each role at least once. If there are four members in your group, use two observers for each session. Each session should take twenty minutes, including feedback.

Client role

As client you will recall your difficult experience and share this, as far as you feel able, with the counsellor. It could be helpful to convey your feelings both at the time of the incident and now.

Counsellor role

As counsellor you will wish to listen to your client. Try to establish the client's feelings, both at the time of the incident and now. Try to help the person discover why the event was difficult for him/her.

How does your client feel about the way in which s/he coped with the situation? Is there perhaps some unfinished business? What pointers are there for the future which arise from the experience?

Observer role

Identify factors which help/hinder:

● the flow of information, feelings and meaning from the client;

● the understanding which the counsellor has of the situation.

How good was the listening? How were pace and direction set? Take a few minutes to feed back your observations, thoughts and perceptions to your group members.

Bibliography

Brammer, L. M., *The Helping Relationship: Process and Skills*, Prentice-Hall, 1978.

Carkhuff, R., *The Art of Helping III*, Human Resource Development Press, 1977.

Edwards, H., *Psychological Problems: Who can help?*, British Psychological Society, 1987.

Egan, G., *The Skilled Helper*, Brooks/Cole, 1975.

Egan, G., *Exercises in Helping Skills*, Brooks/Cole, 1975.

Reddy, M., *The Manager's Guide to Counselling at Work*, British Psychological Society, 1987.

17

Counselling empathy scale

Description

This activity provides an opportunity for participants to practise and strengthen counselling skills through role play exercises focusing particularly on empathizing.

Situations

The activity is suitable for groups of six to twenty-four participants as part of a programme covering counselling, management development or occupational groups who are involved in counselling.

Objectives

- To develop understanding and awareness of the different levels of empathy in counselling.
- To enable participants to assess their own counselling skills against the counselling empathy scale.
- To strengthen approaches to counselling.

Trainer guidance

The central part of the activity focuses on role plays in groups of three. The participant playing the role of client will ideally produce their own problem or issue to form the basis of the counselling interview but you may wish to establish some ground rules to ensure that these problems are appropriate, or, as an alternative, to provide some scenarios for participants to work with.

Feedback from the observers of the role plays is important and you may need to brief observers carefully to ensure that feedback is presented in a positive, constructive manner.

Method

1. A scale that is helpful for establishing how people can achieve empathy has been developed. It has been found useful to rate counsellor empathy on five different levels. The higher the level on the scale the more empathic understanding we can communicate to others. This helps individuals to discover and use their own resources.

    Distribute Handout 17.1 to participants and ask them to examine it in the light of their previous experience.

    Then set up role plays to examine at which levels of empathic understanding they are communicating. You should aim to achieve as much empathy as possible. The first step in doing so is to identify the typical level of empathy used by participants.

2. The role plays should consider a serious problem or current concern. You will need groups of at least three for this: one person practising empathy, the second playing the person being interviewed, the third or more people participating as observers.

    The observer's role is to score the role play on the level of empathic understanding displayed by the interviewer. You should use several role plays, switching so that each person gets a chance to play all three roles. Try to ensure that the issues raised are relevant and of current concern to participants.

3. Familiarize participants with the Counselling Empathy Scale (Handout 17.1) and its uses in the various role plays and scenarios. Ask the observers to score the level of counselling involvement on different levels of the empathy scale for any particular scenario. Then discuss the skill of the interviewer with the participants and how different levels of empathy detract from or add to the counselling process. Make a particular point of focusing on how different levels of empathy play a key role in the management of human resources in personal and working life. A number of points are worth making here:

    - You should help the group to establish that feeling understood increases the liking of interviewees for interviewers.
    - Feeling understood, interviewees come to trust themselves more under these circumstances.

- Feeling understood facilitates interviewees' confidence in exploring the problem and themselves further.
- Finally, feeling understood provides the interviewee with a basis for considering alternative action and taking it.

4. *Feedback/summary:* In counselling, empathy is the key skill for freeing human resources. Its explicit communication, particularly during early counselling contact, is critical. Without a sufficient level of empathy and understanding there is a poor foundation for people making significant changes in their personal and working lives.

Timing

1. Introduction and setting up the role plays takes five to ten minutes.

2. Running the role plays takes one hour to one hour fifteen minutes.

3. Feedback takes thirty minutes.

Average total time: one and a half hours.

Materials

1. Sufficient copies of Handout 17.1.

2. Sufficient space for groups to work undisturbed.

3. Flipchart, paper and pens.

Counselling empathy scale

Level one (score 1)

The verbal and behavioural expressions or non-verbal expressions of the interviewer either do not attend to or significantly detract from the verbal and behavioural expressions of the interviewee, so that they communicate significantly less of the person's feelings and experiences than the person has communicated to him/herself.

> *Example.* The interviewer communicates no awareness of even the most obvious expressed surface feelings or behaviours of the interviewee. The interviewer may be bored or disinterested or simply operating from a preconceived framework or reference point which totally excludes the interviewee.

SUMMARY

The interviewer does everything but express that he/she is listening, understanding, hearing or being sensitive, even to the most obvious feelings and behaviours of the interviewee in such a way as to significantly detract from the counselling that is taking place. In other words, he/she is actually detracting from the communications that exist between him/herself and the other person.

Level two (score 2)

The interviewer responds to the expressed feelings and behaviours of the interviewee but does so in such a way that he/she actually detracts noticeably from the communication with him/her.

> *Example.* The interviewer may communicate some awareness of obvious surface feelings or behaviours of the interviewee but his/her communication drains off to a level where it actually distorts the behaviour, the affect, or the level of meaning that is being communicated. The interviewer may actually communicate his/her own ideas of what is going on but these are not congruent with the expressions of the interviewee.

SUMMARY

The interviewer clearly tends to respond to his/her own view rather than that which the interviewee is expressing or indicating in his/her behaviour.

Level three (score 3)

The interviewer's expressions are in response to the expressions of the interviewee. These are essentially interchangeable with those of the other person in that they express fundamentally the surface thinking, emotion, behaviour and meaning intended by them.

Example. The interviewer responds with accurate understanding of the surface feelings and behaviours of the interviewee but he/she may not respond to, or he/she may actually misinterpret the deeper feelings and behaviours and thinking of the other person.

SUMMARY

The interviewer at level three is responding so as neither to subtract from nor add to the expressions and behaviours of the interviewee. But he/she does not respond accurately to how that person really feels and thinks *beneath* the surface. The interviewer instead indicates a willingness and openness to do so but just fails to achieve this level of understanding.

Level four (score 4)

Here the interviewer's responses *noticeably add* to the expressions, thinking, feelings and behaviour of the interviewee in such a way as to express a deeper level of understanding that is shared between the interviewer and the interviewee.

> *Example.* The interviewer communicates his/her understanding of the expressions of the interviewee at a level deeper than they were expressed by the person being interviewed and thus enables him/her to experience and express a state or thoughts and feelings he/she may have been unable to previously.

SUMMARY

At level four empathy interviewers are able to provide responses that add deeper feeling and meaning to the expressions of interviewees. In other words, level four empathy gets to 'the heart of the matter' and identifies issues that are of genuine concern to individuals. Employing empathy at this level usually produces impressive results.

Level five (score 5)

The interviewer operating at level five adds significantly to the thinking, feelings, meanings, expressions and behaviour of the interviewee in such a way as to accurately express feelings at a deeper level than the interviewee him/herself would normally be able to express, and in so doing helps the interviewee to gain a greater self-exploration and deeper understanding of his/her problems. At this level the interviewer is 'fully with' the interviewee in uncovering the core of the problem.

> *Example:* The interviewer responds with accurate empathy at level five to *all* of the interviewee's deeper as well as surface feelings, thoughts and behaviour. In all these departments, the interviewer is 'tuned in' to the interviewee's wavelength. This is what 'fine-tuning' means. At this level the interviewer and the interviewee can proceed together to explore previously unexplored areas and the use of their human resources in the face of current concerns and personal and occupational demands.

SUMMARY

Operating at level five the interviewer is responding with full awareness of who the other person is, and with a comprehensive and accurate empathic understanding of the interviewee's deepest feelings, thoughts, behaviours, problems and aspirations.

18

Combining counselling skills

Description

This activity involves participants in working on a series of short case studies based on counselling situations.

Situations

The activity may be used on a counselling course or on any training programme where counselling or problem solving is covered. The activity is suitable for groups of six to sixteen people.

Objectives

- To enable participants to strengthen the skills of responding to problems using empathy and probing techniques.

- To provide an opportunity to practise empathy and probing responses.

Trainer guidance

Combining empathy with probing is a powerful way of helping people to find the courage to tackle their problems at work. Empathy with probing tells people that we really care about them but we are not going to accept the situation at its face value. Combining empathy with probing permits managers to be both caring and critical.

Method

1. Introduce the exercise by explaining that the objective of the activity is to learn the skill of replying to a person with empathy and then following it up with a probe. This is called empathy probing.

2. Ask participants to decide what kind of information or clarification they require when working with people. They should see this in terms of concrete and specific experiences, behaviours and cognitions. These should be used to help the individual see the problem more clearly. Distribute Handout 18.1 and use the case study examples to cue participants into combined counselling skills. Allow participants to work on the case studies in pairs or small groups.

3. Call participants back into a plenary session and review responses to the case studies. Ask participants to discuss how they communicated the empathy responses and the way probing was used. Ensure that a complete and satisfactory discussion is held to decide the various issues surrounding the practical development of empathic response and probing skills.

4. Note any corrective coaching that is required for individual participants.

5. Conclude by asking for the views of participants on the use of empathy combined with probing as a set of counselling skills. Raise and discuss any remaining issues over the practice of these skills. Summarize the possible range of applications they may have at work. End by going over the main points on a flipchart or overhead projector slide.

Timing

1. Introducing the exercise and explaining empathy probing techniques takes fifteen minutes.

2. The case studies take thirty to forty minutes.

3. Feedback and conclusion takes thirty minutes.

Total average time: one hour fifteen minutes.

Materials

1. Sufficient copies of Handout 18.1.

2. Sufficient space for participants to work undisturbed.

3. Flipchart, paper and marker pens.

4. Overhead projector – optional.

Empathy – probing case studies

Example

A member of staff who has been studying for a management qualification on part-time day release is talking to you.

> 'I found out yesterday that I have failed the first year and there is no way I can carry on. I've seen everybody but the path is blocked this time. It's a real mess. I've no idea how I'll face my manager and the staff team – two of them wanted day release and didn't get it. On top of that my partner has such high expectations of me. Everyone has given me support and the Department has spent a great deal of time and money on this course. I suppose I'll have to tell them now that it's all wasted.'

Empathy response

> 'You seem to be saying the situation seems pretty grim now, both at work and at home. Everything sounds so final.'

Probing questions

- What is needed to make the situation more concrete and clear?

- Who did the staff member actually see?

- Precisely what sort of refusals or responses did s/he get?

Probing response

> 'I wonder if you could help me understand this a bit better – I'm not quite clear what you mean by everybody and the obstacles that are in your way.'

In this example the use of empathy and probing skills helps to check whether the person actually did think of all the possibilities before reaching the conclusion that s/he has done. Using combined empathy–probing skills we share in how the staff member actually feels, but still check the accuracy of the conclusions. This is why probing is necessary.

Case study 1

A woman in a senior professional position is talking to you about trouble with her partner's father.

> 'The truth as I see it is that he is interfering so much in my personal life that it is affecting my work. He is so understanding and yet he is so cunning and clever. I find it very hard just to know what he is doing. But I come to work and I just can't seem to concentrate any more. So subtle. I suppose I'm finished. I don't know if I can hold down the job any longer. I suppose I'm getting close to quitting and giving up all together. He keeps sending me flowers.'

What are appropriate empathy responses? What probing questions seem appropriate? How will you combine empathy with probing? Script it and role play.

Empathy response

Probing questions

Probing response

Case study 2

A woman administrator is talking to you.

'I just can't stand my job any more. I find my team leader so unreasonable. There are all sorts of ludicrous, outrageous and totally unreasonable demands on me. The other women in the office are so stuffy I can't even talk to them. And the men are so boring and sexist and after you all the time – you know what I mean? I suppose that salary and conditions are OK but I don't think that makes up for all the rest of the things I've got to manage and cope with. It's hard to believe that this has been going on for almost two years.'

Empathy response

Probing questions

Probing response

Case study 3

A divorced man is talking to you at work about his drinking. He has just finished telling his story.

> 'To be frank, it's a relief to tell someone. I don't have to make any excuses or tell any stories to you – make the story fit or try to make it sound right. It's quite simple. I drink because I like to drink. I'm mad about alcohol. That's all. So I'm not fooling myself. Telling you isn't going to solve it either. Because, when I get out of here, I can tell you, I go straight to a pub and drink and drink and drink. It's got to be some new bar where there are new faces and everything is unfamiliar – a place where they don't know me.'

Empathy response

Probing questions

Probing responses

Case study 4

A man who has just undergone surgery that has left him with one lung is talking to you at work.

> 'I'll never be as active again as I used to be. I realize that now – something I've had to face up to – but at least I'm beginning to see life is worth living. I've taken a long hard look at myself. I have to take a look at the possibilities no matter how much they might have narrowed down. I can't explain how this happened, but there's something of the good feelings stirring in me. I'm not sure if I can be the senior manager I used to be. Maybe all that will have to be behind me now.'

Empathy response

Probing questions

Probing response

19

Going for goals

Description

This activity enables participants to develop realistic goals/targets through a practical exercise based on a counselling or problem-solving discussion.

Situations

The activity is useful for managers or staff involved in establishing targets or goals. It may be used as part of a training programme related to change, performance improvement, counselling, or as part of a team-building programme.

This is an excellent activity for managers to use with their staff groups. It can be used for pairs or groups of six to ten people. Adjustments to the process may need to be made, depending on whether the activity is run by the manager or by a trainer and depending on the numbers involved.

Objectives

- To enable participants to identify goals/targets that are specific, measurable and realistic.

- To demonstrate the importance of joint development of goals/targets.

Trainer guidance

Goal setting is a central part of counselling and performance management and managers should be aware of it as a means of establishing preferred

163

outcomes with colleagues and team members. It is a collaborative process between the manager and each individual. This is a process in which you do not impose your views on people. It is not the manager's views that are important but the *collaboration*, maximizing the probability of problems being clearly identified and goals being created in specific terms. As managers or counsellors, your task is to help the person examine and identify relevant goals and clarify specifically the way they might be attained. The motivation to attain goals is likely to be much greater if people perceive that the goals are right for them. A rule of thumb is that if the person has no motivation or a great lack of motivation it may be manifested in 'dropping out' or resisting. Another sign is that they may not complete their job assignments. Once managers have begun to set goals together with their staff, an explicit contract is formed between the manager and the individual. Both parties should be committed to, and agree to cooperate to the best of their ability, to attain the goals agreed.

It is helpful to write down the goals that are to be achieved. The manager can do this but it is better for individuals to write their own goals and keep a copy to remind them of the goals they have agreed. Some contracts for goals are written so specifically that they include not only the goals but the individual's obligation in meeting them. It is not unusual for such contracts to be signed by both the manager and the staff member. Where there are several goals, managers may need to work with the staff member to assign priorities. Rank ordering them in terms of their importance is a useful approach. Two important considerations here are the degree to which they are contributing specifically to the individual's conduct and if there are any time constraints. For example, there may be a goal to attend three team meetings a month which is in competition with the goal of attending complaints committee meetings. Goals should not be rigid but flexible, allowing change. The original goals set may need to be reformulated as the management or counselling process continues.

Method

1. This assignment can be carried out in a number of ways – individually, in pairs, or with all participants as one group.

2. *Individually.* Ask the individual to assess and analyse a problem drawn from his/her own life experience or from a current concern at work. Write out the goals in relation to this problem.

    - State them in behavioural terms.
    - Make them specific and measurable.
    - Make them realistic.
    - Tailor the goals to the individual's own concern.

3. *In pairs:* Work with Handout 19.1 and instruct each pair to counsel their partner about a problem either drawn from their own experience or a current concern at work. Stimulate and role play these experiences. After the problem has been clarified in collaboration with their partners, explain and discuss the principles of setting goals, and then together formulate the goals for subsequent counselling sessions. Again:

   - State them in behavioural terms.
   - Make them specific and measurable.
   - Make them realistic.
   - Tailor the goals to the individual concerned.

   Before concluding the session discuss and formulate the kind of contract which will be most appropriate for subsequent sessions.

4. *All participants as one group:* Carry out similar activities, asking participants to choose a significant problem they want to work on and one in which they need to set goals for themselves. Then reverse roles, so that the manager becomes the employee and the employee becomes the manager. You can give a demonstration interview of setting goals, using a participant as an employee.

5. *Feedback/summary:* Hold a plenary session in which all participants present and receive feedback about the goals they have formulated, the assignments they carried out and their perceptions of the goal-setting session. Pay particular attention to the importance of the four criteria for goal setting:

   - Whether they were set in behavioural terms.
   - Whether they were specific and measurable.
   - Whether they were realistic.
   - Whether they were tailored and 'owned' by the individual concerned.

   Encourage participants to explore these issues extensively and record relevant items on a flipchart or overhead projector slide. After participants complete their goal setting, ask them what they learned from it.

Timing

1. Introducing the exercise and formulating goals takes forty minutes.

2. Feedback takes twenty to forty minutes, depending on the number of participants.

Materials

1. Sufficient copies of Handout 19.1.

2. Sufficient space for participants to work undisturbed.

3. Flipchart, paper and marker pens.

Goal-setting inventory

Goal	Relevant description/specification	Time frame (date to be achieved)
1.		
2.		
3.		
4.		
5.		

20

Fishbone that problem

Description

This particular activity suggests an approach for the group to take in order to solve or break down a problem.

Situations

'Fishboning' is especially relevant for training sessions with a brainstorming, planning, or structured group approach to a specific situation.

Objectives

- To suggest a structured approach to solving problems.

- To help participants adopt a disciplined technique as part of the planning process.

Trainer guidance

There are no particular pitfalls for the trainer to be wary of. However, as with any such exercise, the trainer should be familiar with how the fishbone works, and the benefits of using it from a participant's point of view.

Method

1. Distribute copies of the blank Fishbone Diagram (Handout 20.1).

2. Explain that the particular business issue or problem to be solved is put at the *Head* of the fishbone.

    The boxes at the end of each bone are the *Key Elements* which make up the topic under review.

    The lines under each box are the *Specific Items* which make up the Key Element in the box.

    The final result is a one-page picture of a particular problem or business issue. The group can use that picture as a basis for short, medium and long term action planning. (See completed diagram on 'How to Improve Customer Service', page 171.)

3. Split participants into groups of four to six, with each group deciding on a subject area it would like to fishbone; for example, to improve staff performance or to cut down on paperwork.

4. Indicate that brainstorming should be used to generate twelve to sixteen potential Key Elements, from which the best six or eight can be chosen.

5. Repeat the brainstorming instruction to identify the best four or five Specific Items from a list of eight or ten.

6. Stress that, if best results are to be achieved, not all the groups' first ideas will be their best.

Timing

The activity is best undertaken in three stages:

1. Group briefing on what fishboning is about takes fifteen minutes.

2. Group work on their own fishbones takes forty-five minutes.

3. Presenting their fishbones and allowing each group to challenge the findings of the other groups takes thirty minutes.

Total time required: approximately one and a half hours.

Materials required

1. Sufficient copies of Handout 20.1.

2. Separate areas for each group to work undisturbed.

3. Flipchart for each group, paper and marker pens.

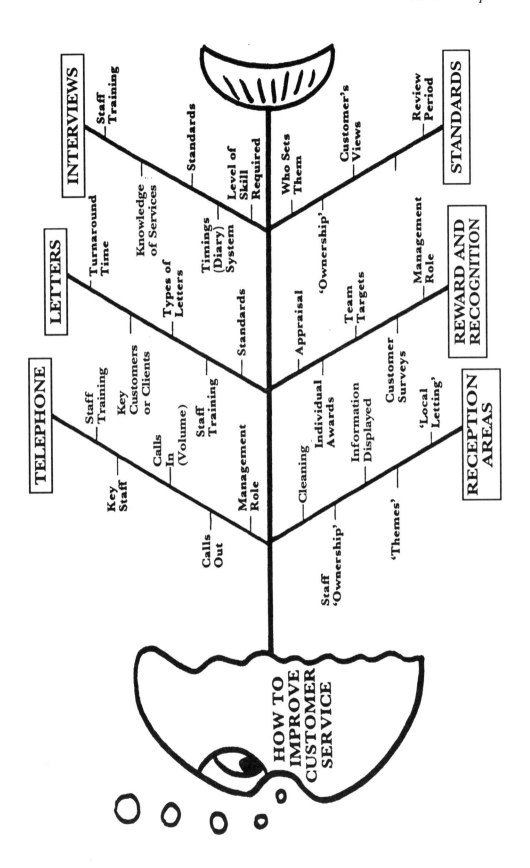

TELEPHONE
- Key Staff
- Staff Training
- Calls In (Volume)
- Key Customers or Clients
- Calls Out
- Staff Training
- Management Role

LETTERS
- Turnaround Time
- Knowledge of Services
- Types of Letters
- Timings (Diary) System
- Standards

INTERVIEWS
- Staff Training
- Standards
- Level of Skill Required
- Who Sets Them
- Customer's Views

STANDARDS
- Review Period

RECEPTION AREAS
- Staff 'Ownership'
- Cleaning
- 'Themes'
- Individual Awards
- Information Displayed
- Customer Surveys
- 'Local Letting'

REWARD AND RECOGNITION
- Appraisal
- 'Ownership'
- Team Targets
- Management Role

HOW TO IMPROVE CUSTOMER SERVICE

Fishbone diagram

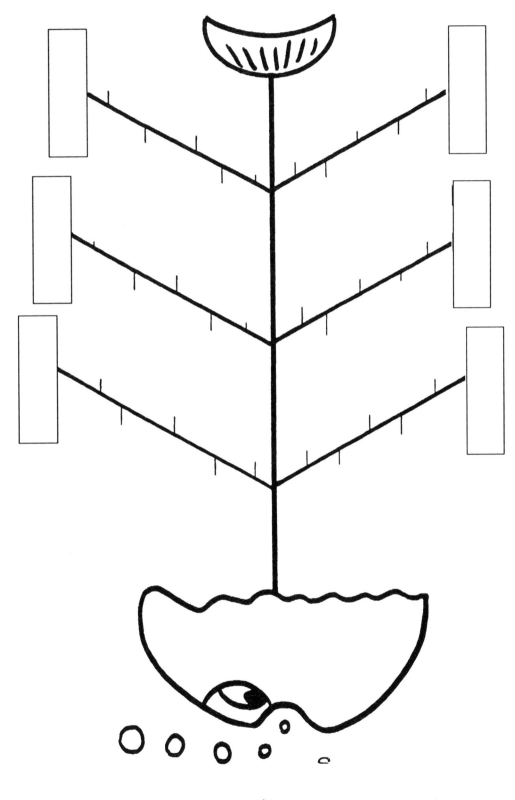

21

Reducing harmful stress

Description

This activity will enable participants to analyse incidents which placed them under severe pressure or stress and which caused great discomfort.

Situations

May be used on its own or as part of a course or workshop programme on the subject of stress. Intended for use by all levels of employee.

Objective

- To reflect upon incidents or situations which placed participants under severe, uncomfortable pressure or stress.

- To suggest possible reasons or underlying causes leading to the stressful condition.

- To seek remedies or options for reducing stress in the future.

Trainer guidance

Much of what has been written on stress is highly subjective and does not lend itself to easy diagnosis. This problem is exacerbated by the fact that experiencing some stress seems to be desirable and that 'stressors' – those factors which act upon us to produce stress – affect different people in different ways and to varying degrees. At the prospect of delivering a public

175

speech, for example, some individuals feel physically sick – while others will rise to the challenge and enjoy it.

The effects of stress can be grouped into two main categories:

(a) *Mental* – tiredness, irritability, anxiousness, sleeplessness, etc.;

(b) *Physical* – indigestion, headaches, palpitations, sweating, etc.

Many stress tests have been produced including the well-known Holmes Rahe Scale which assigns high scores to traumatic events such as the death of a loved one or divorce with lesser scores to everyday events such as changes in working hours.

This activity does not set out to evaluate stress in a medical or academic way. Its main purpose is to promote discussion of the subject; to enable participants to share experiences, feelings and views aided by a structured exercise. You can do much to wean participants away from the expectation that this activity will provide a 'cure-all'. Instead, the emphasis needs to be on raising awareness and understanding that stress is a perfectly natural state which all people experience.

Method

1. Send each participant a copy of Handout 21.1 (Stress Review) *ten days* in advance of the scheduled programme, together with an invitation to complete it before the session. Inform participants that their cooperation is valued and will enhance the levels of interest and participation during the course.

2. After a brief introduction, divide participants into two or three groups and give them the following tasks.

    Task A
    Ask each participant to give a brief description of his/her stressful incident as recorded on Handout 21.1. While each account is being given, other members should listen carefully.

    Task B
    When all participants have finished their accounts, ask each group to discuss the points from these incidents. Distribute Handout 21.2 and ask groups to produce two flipcharts as instructed.

3. Bring participants together and ask each group's representative to give feedback, using the prepared flipcharts which should be displayed side by side.

4. When all presentations have been made, lead a general discussion on the issues raised. Useful areas for discussion are:

- The diversity of situations and the different perceptions about what constitutes stress.
- The wide range of coping and stress-reduction methods.
- The spectrum of normal feelings associated with stress.
- The increased understanding and potential learning when individuals are prepared to trust others with their accounts of stressful situations.

Encourage participants to discuss and consider the likelihood that at least one of the stress reduction methods listed will help in *every* situation.

5. Ask participants to record key points about their learning from the activity and share these in their groups.

Timing

1. Completing Handout 21.1 should take between fifteen and thirty minutes.

2. Sharing incidents and completing Handout 21.2 takes forty to sixty minutes.

3. Presentations take twenty to thirty minutes.

4. Discussion takes twenty to thirty minutes.

5. Recording and sharing key learning points takes ten to fifteen minutes.

Average total time: two hours.

Materials required

1. Sufficient copies of Handouts 21.1 and 21.2.

2. Sufficient space for groups to work undisturbed.

3. Flipchart paper and pens.

Stress review sheet

1. Briefly describe an incident or situation which caused you severe pressure/discomfort/stress.

2. In one or two words describe how you felt as a result of this incident. In the box below are some examples of descriptive words to help you:

> fine, grand, lovely, perfect, brilliant, happy, relaxed, calm, confident, angry, subdued, humiliated, funny, peculiar, awful, terrible, tired, weary, exhausted, weak, frightened, scared, petrified, uncomfortable sick, sweaty, cold, hot, ill, alone, hurt, disgraced, incompetent, silly.

3. On a scale of 1 to 10 record how well you think you 'coped' with this incident.

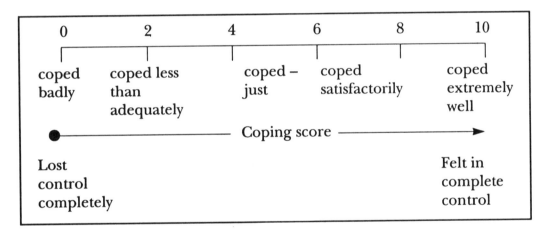

Incident (1)	I felt ... (2)	Coping score (3)

4. Finally, describe some methods you could usefully employ to *reduce* your personal stress should any similar incident occur.

Task B – preparing flipcharts

Select one member of your group to take on the responsibility for feeding back your group's findings to the other groups when reassembled. You should produce two flipcharts as follows:

CHART 1

Examples of incidents (1)	How did you feel? (2)	Coping score (3)	Stress reduction method number (4)

(a) List all, or a good number, of the incidents reported by participants in column 1.

(b) Record each individual's descriptive 'feeling' word(s) in column 2.

(c) Record each individual's coping score in column 3.

CHART 2

Make a numbered list of all the stress reduction/coping methods identified by your group.

Finally, complete column 4 of Chart 1 by taking each incident in turn and discussing which of the coping methods might be employed for that situation should it occur again. The appropriate numbered method from Chart 2 is recorded in column 4.

22

Agenda

Description

In this activity a series of short meetings help identify the essential components of chairing successful meetings. The trainer builds on the participants' own ideas, thereby dealing with the subject in a practical manner.

Situations

This activity is useful in the development of chairing skills. It can also be used as a team-building exercise or for examining communication techniques.

Objectives

- To identify the preparation necessary to conduct successful meetings.

- To demonstrate the different character types who attend meetings and how to deal effectively with them.

- To help participants ensure that meetings reach a conclusion.

Trainer guidance

1. The trainer must not participate in the meetings unless clarification of the agenda time is required.

2. Notes should be taken of attitudes and incidents which can be reviewed in the concluding discussion.

Method

1. Make no preparations as for a meeting. Let participants decide on the seating arrangements.

2. Display the first agenda item (Handout 22.1) and explain that the group has fifteen minutes to discuss and agree its views.

3. After fifteen minutes elicit the group's views and list them on a flipchart (if a member has not done this already).

4. Repeat the process for the second and third agenda items. Ensure that the group incorporates any earlier learning points into their discussions.

5. The group should be encouraged to offer the chairing role to various members so that as many as possible can gain the practical experience of leading a meeting.

Timing

With each meeting taking a maximum of fifteen minutes, at least twenty minutes should then be allowed to collate and discuss the views of the group on each item. The timescale can be varied by the trainer depending upon the depth to which the subject is explored.

Materials required

1. Sufficient copies of Handout 22.1.

2. A flipchart on which to record the views of the group, paper and pens.

Internal memorandum

Date: (of meeting)

Reference: (who called the meeting)

Location: (where the meeting is)

Subject:

AGENDA

1. What essential steps of planning and preparation will help a meeting to be successful? (fifteen minutes)

2. How can a chairperson deal with the different types of personalities present at a meeting? (fifteen minutes)

3. How can a chairperson gain the commitment of all participants and ensure that the meeting reaches a conclusion? (fifteen minutes)

23

Brief moments

Description

This activity involves participants attending a meeting and transferring the information gained into a format suitable for team briefing. Using role play, one member must brief a staff team accordingly.

Situations

As the activity involves attending a meeting and holding a team briefing it can be beneficial on a variety of training events, such as those dealing with inter-personal skills, communication skills or team building. The activity is also useful for programmes dealing with change management, where managers need to keep staff teams fully informed of the changes taking place.

Objectives

- To identify the key elements of a meeting and convey them to team members.
- To practise the team briefing process.
- To develop communication skills.

Trainer guidance

This activity has most impact if the subject of the initial meeting/presentation is relevant to the participants' current areas of work.

Since the trainer makes the initial presentation, s/he needs to have a very good understanding of the topic and be able to answer questions on it.

Trainers should select the subject for the initial meeting, ensuring that it includes some information from each of the key areas – Policy, People, Progress, Points for Action (see Handout 23.1).

Method

Give participants a full briefing before the start of the activity. This is of utmost importance.

1. Give a copy of Handout 23.1 to each individual and explain the concept of team briefing. Cover the following points:

    (i)   The subjects chosen should be relevant to all team members.
    (ii)   Individual topics or grievances should not be discussed.
    (iii) Team briefings should be a regular aspect of team management; they do not replace the normal communication process – they supplement it.

2. Explain that you are about to brief the participants on a topic and that they should take notes during the presentation. Encourage them to ask questions at the end.

3. Give the presentation, which should last at least ten minutes; include elements from each of the four key areas: Policy, Progress, People and Points for Action.

4. Following the presentation and questions, allow the delegates to transfer their notes into the format shown on Handout 23.1. Fifteen minutes should be sufficient for this purpose.

5. Then divide the group into teams of four. Ask one from each team to brief the other three on the original presentation. Then request the other members to comment on the items covered in the briefing and whether any important points were missed.

6. Reconvene the whole group and discuss the value of this type of team briefing.

Timing

1. The initial briefing will take twenty minutes.

2. The presentation and questions session will also take twenty minutes.

3. Allow participants up to fifteen minutes to transfer their notes on to

Handout 23.1.

4. Allow twenty minutes to role play the team briefing and then discuss it.

Total time required: approximately seventy-five minutes.

Materials required

1. Sufficient copies of Handout 23.1.
2. Scrap paper (for note taking).

Team briefing

Date: ....   Start time: ....

Attended by: ....   Finish time: ....

....

....

....

AGENDA

1. *Policy* (decisions taken which affect the team members' area of operation):

2. *Progress* (the progress which has been made or is to be made):

3. *People* (the effect on team members):

4. *Points for Action* (specific action to be carried out by team members):

Notes   (points raised at the Team Briefing)

24

The message was ...

Description

This is an exercise based on the old game of Chinese Whispers. It involves individuals passing on a specific message which, through a series of transmissions, becomes distorted.

Situations

This practical communications exercise is useful for any course concerned with listening or communication skills.

Objectives

- To highlight the importance of clear communication.

- To emphasize the benefits of *actively listening*. To show how the *grapevine* can grow with distorted information.

Trainer guidance

There are no real pitfalls in this exercise. However, the trainer must remember the following points in relation to the second part of the activity.

1. Position the exercise so that the participants do not begin to rationalize the reality of the situation in passing on a particular message.
2. The exercise must begin with the group work on listening, from which

participants will gain some insight into the penalties in store for people who do not listen.

3. Make sure that all the participants are clear about where they have to be during the second part of the activity, from whom they should receive the message, plus of course, to whom they should give it.

Method

1. Explain the objectives of the session.

2. Divide the group into teams of five or six and give each participant a copy of the Participants' Brief (Handout 24.1); ask them to complete the exercise.

3. Bring the groups together and display their answers on the flipchart. Discuss and clarify the points they make.

4. Introduce the second stage of the exercise by distributing Participants' Brief 2 (Handout 24.2).

5. Allocate a role to everyone in the group. Numbers permitting, you will need two deputy managers, four senior supervisors and eight or so clerical officers. Enter names on Handout 24.2. Assign each person to their own room and enter its number on the Brief.

6. Distribute Participants' Brief 3 (Handout 24.3). Ask the participants to go to their designated rooms/areas and wait for a message from their line management. Remind everyone that it is not possible to take notes.

7. When all the clerical officers and senior supervisors have gone, read the following message to the two deputy managers.

    'I'm sorry I can't stay longer but I'm in a rush so you'll have to tell the staff what I'm going to tell you. It has been decided that only four Grade 3s can attend the estate managers' meeting on the 6th. It's been put back two weeks because of the weather.'

    As the deputy managers are leaving, shout out the following as an after-thought:

    'Oh, by the way, Jayne is getting better and can have visitors from Monday if any one wants to go.'

8. When individuals are going to their next in line to convey the message, stop them and start discussing various aspects of the course, their job, how are they finding the rest of the group etc. This will add to their confusion and test their memory.

NB   No notes can be made – the exercise is totally oral.

9. When everyone has returned, ask the clerical officers to write down, without discussion, what they believe the message was. Then one by one ask each clerical officer confidentially the six questions indicated on the grid below which should have been drawn in advance on the flipchart.

QUESTIONS	CLERKS' NAMES	→	→	→	→	ANSWERS
Who can go to the meeting?						4 Grade 3s
What staff group is concerned?						Estate managers
When is the conference?						6th
Who decided who could go to the conference?						'IT'
Why was the conference put back?						The weather
When can you visit Jayne?						From Monday

10. Chart the clerical officers' answers to the six questions and indicate whether correct or not. The maximum number of correct answers is the number of clerical officers times six.

11. From the answers given, work out how many *incorrect* or incomplete messages were given.

12. Chair a general discussion on what this exercise has demonstrated to the group.

Timing

The whole exercise should take about forty minutes: twenty minutes for the 'message passing' section, and twenty minutes for analysis and discussion.

Materials required

1. Many individually 'designated' areas or rooms, if possible with distance between them.

2. Flipchart (for grid), paper and pens.

3. Sufficient copies of Handouts 24.1, 24.2 and 24.3

Participants' brief 1

As a group, discuss the following question and be prepared to nominate a spokesperson to give the views of your team.

WHAT ARE THE PENALTIES TO (a) the individual and (b) the organization OF PEOPLE NOT LISTENING ATTENTIVELY?

You have twenty minutes to complete the exercise.

HOW THE INDIVIDUAL SUFFERS	*HOW THE ORGANIZATION SUFFERS*

Participants' brief 2

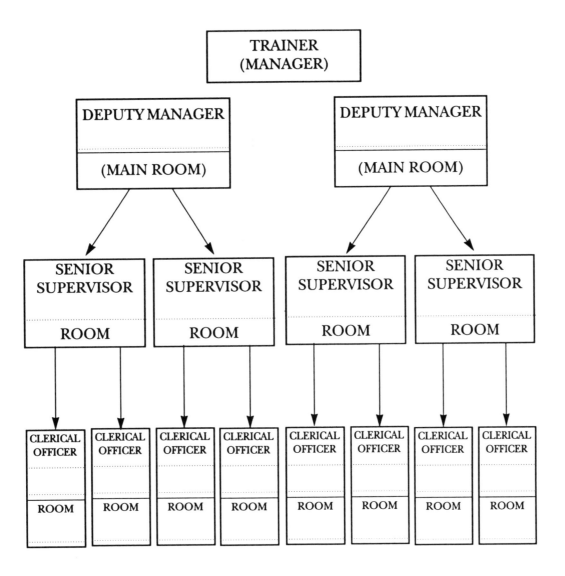

All the designated areas/rooms should be different and if possible well separated.

Participants' brief 3

You are all members of a department which is very scattered in terms of office accommodation, necessitating a heavy reliance on oral communication. Your manager (the trainer) will give the two deputy managers a message. Each will pass it to the two senior supervisors in their team. Since they occupy separate rooms, each will have to convey the message twice. Each senior supervisor will repeat the message to however many clerical officers there are in the team, whose offices are widely scattered. When they have received the message, the clerical officers will return to the main room and write down what they believe the message was. No discussion is permitted among department members at any stage. Nor may any notes be taken.

25

Just stick to the facts

Description

This activity illustrates the difference between facts, judgements and irrelevant information. Initially the groups produce a definition for each. Syndicate group work follows with each group analysing news events as recorded in a current daily newspaper, assessing how many facts, judgements and pieces of irrelevant information are included.

Situations

This is a short, practical exercise which can be used to highlight the need for factual information in such situations as planning for change, assessing performance, handling complaints and investigations etc.

Objectives

- To understand the difference between facts, judgements and irrelevant information.

- To discuss the importance of using factual information in a range of management activities.

Trainer guidance

This activity was originally designed for use in appraisal training but can easily be used in the wider range of situations suggested above.

There is currently much interest in managing performance both through monitoring and appropriate management action on performance problems. The activity is likely to be of use in training programmes dealing with any of these issues. Participants may also wish to discuss the problems of obtaining factual information on performance where performance measures are difficult to identify – such as interpersonal skills and many aspects of working with people.

Method

1. In advance of the activity, write these headings on three separate pieces of flipchart:

    - A fact is:
    - A judgement is:
    - Irrelevant information is:

2. Outline the objectives of the activity and ask the group to define collectively the three headings listed on the flipchart. Possible definitions are:

    - A fact is an event which is verifiable from experience or observation.
    - A judgement is a deduction or viewpoint.
    - Irrelevant information is data or material unconcerned with the matter in hand.

3. Divide the participants into two groups and give each group the same selection of articles from a current newspaper. Explain that each group should use the definitions on the flipchart to decide which sections of the article fall into which category. Allow fifteen minutes for this.

4. Review the exercise by examining each group's suggestions and comparing the differences between the two groups.

5. Ask the groups to consider what personal opinion the writer had on the issue. Stress that it is very easy to work out the personal opinion of a writer if the article is composed of a high percentage of judgements.

6. Stress that views expressed on any aspect of performance assessment (or the activity you wish to relate the exercise to) should be based on factual information. Assessment based on facts is generally accepted by the staff member as the information normally cannot be disputed. Ask the group where they will be able to obtain such factual information. Answers could include:

    - Working alongside the individual.
    - Consulting others.
    - Referring to formal records.

- Recording information throughout the assessment period.

Point out that irrelevant information is often included to add to the length of an assessment or a report. This serves no useful purpose and often indicates that the assessment or investigation has not been thoroughly conducted and that factual information is lacking.

7. Summarize the key points of the session.

Timing

1. Introducing the exercise and definitions takes ten minutes.

2. Group work takes fifteen minutes.

3. Discussion and summary take fifteen minutes.

Total average time: forty minutes.

Materials

1. Flipchart and pens.

2. Sufficient copies of a current newspaper.

26

Is anybody listening?

Description

This activity is a practical listening exercise which examines the benefits of accurate listening, the costs of not listening and the skills needed to become a 'good listener'.

Situations

The activity is appropriate for a wide range of individual and group activities where listening is important. The size of the group can be anything from six to twenty-four people.

Objectives

- To practise active listening.

- To enable participants to practise and assess their listening skills.

- To develop action plans for strengthening listening skills.

Trainer guidance

This is a straightforward activity which should not present any particular problems. If you wish to focus the exercise on listening in any specific situations you can ask the participants to identify issues relevant to these situations in stage 2 of the method – for example, issues related to change or to performance difficulties.

Method

1. Divide participants into twos or threes. In the groups of two there is a listener and an 'employee'. In the groups of three there is a listener, an employee and an observer.

2. The participant in the role of the employee should talk about a problem or issues of current concern to her/him, and the observer feeds back to the listener the listening skills s/he was or was not using with the employee. Distribute and use Handout 26.1 to guide the activity. The assignment should run for five to ten minutes.

3. At the end of the activity, the listener should summarize for the employee what s/he was saying and what the listener 'heard'. Ask the employee to comment on the accuracy of the feedback. Then compare and discuss the observations, thoughts and feelings in the small groups.

4. Now ask participants to reverse roles. Repeat the activity until each participant has played each role, discussing any issues that arise. Audio or video recording can be used to provide constructive feedback.

5. Feed back the views of the participants – emphasize the importance of using consistent listening. Note any unhelpful habits of the listener, particularly those which can block communications – and how employee responses can be inhibited by using additional words that are unnecessary in the counselling process. You should also ensure that the participants appreciate the need to discipline themselves to use good listening skills consistently.

Timing

1. Introduction and setting up groups takes five minutes.

2. Group work takes twenty to twenty-five minutes.

3. Feedback and discussion takes fifteen to thirty minutes.

Total average time: fifty minutes.

Materials

1. Sufficient copies of Handout 26.1.

2. Sufficient space for groups to work undisturbed.

3. Flipchart, paper and marker pens.

Listening skills inventory

The main listening skills are:

I know when I am listening well because:

I know when I am not listening well because:

Things I must do to improve my listening skills:

1.

2.

3.

4.

5.

27

Let me explain

Description

This is a practical exercise designed to show the importance of clear and concise language. Working in pairs, one group of participants has to write a series of instructions on how to complete a specific task such as tying a tie. These instructions are carried out by another group who criticize the format and language.

Situations

This is a group activity suitable for all levels. It can be used in any situation in which writing skills are relevant. The activity is also useful for raising energy levels while learning about effective writing.

Objectives

- To give participants the opportunity to produce clear and concise written instructions.
- To receive feedback on the format and language of the written instructions.
- To produce guidelines for effective writing.

Trainer guidance

This activity was originally designed for appraisal training and focused on the writing of appraisal reports. It can easily be adapted to cover any situations in which effective writing skills are important.

Method

1. Before the activity starts, write each of the specific tasks on a separate card.

2. Give a brief introduction to the activity by explaining that this exercise highlights the important of good writing techniques.

3. Divide the group into pairs. Give each pair a card indicating a specific task from the following list:

    -   Lacing a shoe.
    -   Tying a tie.
    -   Playing snap.
    -   Playing noughts and crosses.
    -   Plaiting hair.

4. Explain that each pair should write a set of instructions to describe exactly how to complete the task they have been given.

5. Once written, arrange for each pair to exchange their instructions. Issue appropriate materials and ask each pair to watch each other carry out their instructions. Stress to the group that when completing the task, they must follow the instructions exactly and not deviate from them.

6. Review the exercise by asking the group what elements of the written instructions helped them and what elements hindered them. (For example, clear format, poor handwriting.)

7. Ask the group to consider this exercise and apply the lessons learned to produce guidelines for effective writing skills. A volunteer from the group could list these on the flipchart. These could include:

    -   Use a clear format.
    -   Make handwriting legible.
    -   Check spelling.
    -   Punctuate correctly.
    -   Use language the receiver will understand.
    -   Avoid jargon.
    -   Avoid abbreviations.
    -   Check understanding.
    -   Consider length.

8. Summarize by stressing that many documents are read by a variety of people, without the opportunity of any discussion to clarify the meaning. It is vital, therefore, to follow these guidelines.

Timing

1. Introducing the exercise, setting up groups and writing instructions takes twenty minutes.

2. Carrying out the tasks following instructions takes ten to fifteen minutes.

3. Discussion takes ten to fifteen minutes.

Total average time: forty-five minutes.

Materials

1. A set of cards detailing the specific tasks.

2. Materials for completing each task, e.g. a tie, a shoe and a lace, playing cards etc.

3. Flipchart, paper and marker pens.

28

Easy listening

Description

This activity involves participants in completing a self-assessment form responding to statements concerning their listening skills. Using this information, the group brainstorm the skills of attentive listening and then practise these skills in groups of three.

Situations

This activity is suitable for any training programme where listening skills or communication skills are covered.

Objectives

- To assess participants' listening skills.
- To practise attentive listening.

Trainer guidance

This activity was initially designed for appraisal training but can be used for any situation where listening is important. If you wish to focus the activity more precisely, Handout 28.1 can be amended to fit with more specialized situations such as counselling, poor performance interviews etc.

Method

1. Begin by distributing Handout 28.1 and explaining that the group will now complete a self-assessment questionnaire to establish their listening skills. Ask participants to imagine themselves in a situation where listening is important and encourage honesty.

2. Encourage the sharing of results within a large group. Ask for specific examples of situations in which participants have listened well or badly. Reinforce those areas where there are similarities within the group.

3. State that there are many facets to the skill of listening, one of the key ones being attentive listening. This means the actual demonstration to the other party that the listener is really listening to what is being said. This mainly incorporates body language with a few words spoken to clarify understanding.

4. Ask the group to think of all those things that would demonstrate attentive listening. Write their answers on the flipchart. Include the following:

    *   Look interested through positive eye contact – not staring or looking away.
    *   Sit forward as if eager to listen.
    *   Use open-hand movements to encourage more information.
    *   Occasionally nod the head to show understanding.
    *   Repeat one or two words that the individual has said, with a questioning tone. This will clarify understanding.
    *   If appropriate, smile.
    *   Use questions that follow on from the conversation that has just taken place.

5. Divide the group into teams of three and ask them to practise some of these attentive skills. There will be three rounds and in each one there will be a speaker, a listener and an observer. Each person should take the opportunity to play each part. The listener should select a topic and a type of person that would particularly bore them and ask the speaker to adopt that person's behaviour and talk on that topic. The listener should practise the attentive skills, watched by the observer.

    At the end of each round, the observer will lead the feedback to the listener, focusing on how successful the listener was in listening attentively. Each round, including feedback, should last a maximum of ten minutes.

6. Review the activity by gathering the thoughts of each group as to how the activity progressed.

7. End the activity by reminding the group of the benefits of listening attentively.

216

Timing

1. The introduction and completing the questionnaire takes fifteen minutes.

2. Discussion of the questionnaire and attentive listening takes ten to fifteen minutes.

3. Group work takes thirty minutes.

4. Final discussion takes fifteen minutes.

Total average time: one hour ten minutes.

Materials

1. Sufficient copies of Handout 28.1.

2. Sufficient space for group work.

3. Flipchart, paper and marker pens.

Listening skills

Read the following statements and tick the box that most applies to your listening skills.

STATEMENTS	ALWAYS	OFTEN	SOMETIMES	NEVER
1. Assume what the speaker is going to say and stop listening.				
2. Look at the speaker while s/he is talking.				
3. Watch what the speaker is saying with words, how it is said with non-verbal movements and the tone of voice used.				
4. Switch off if the speaker is repetitious.				
5. Appear that you are listening even if you are not.				
6. Ask questions to clarify your understanding.				
7. Ask a leading question to get the answer you want.				
8. Sit forward and look as if you are listening.				
9. Listen to the other's viewpoint.				
10. Think about the question you want to ask before the speaker has finished the sentence.				
11. Take notes while the speaker is talking.				
12. Get distracted by your own thoughts.				
13. Restate what the speaker has said to confirm understanding.				
14. Play with pens, draw etc. while the speaker is talking.				
15. Concentrate, if the speaker is boring.				

29

The glass of life

Description

In this activity a list of 'jobs to be done' is discussed by participants with a view to identifying the short and longer term implications of their decisions.

Situations

This activity is effective in getting people to think through a situation using a variety of possible situations. Influencing skills, assertiveness and chairing skills will all be stressed.

Objectives

- To focus attention on setting personal priorities.

- To reinforce the need for 'best' management practices in day-to-day situations.

- To show the importance of taking both a short and long term view of solutions.

Trainer guidance

This activity would complement a general *time management* session. It is a very good introduction to priority setting and action planning (short/long term), underlining the need to look at both domestic and work pressures together.

Participants can then make the connection from the tasks and pressures given in the exercise to those they are currently experiencing.

Method

1. Explain the objectives of the exercise (as outlined above). If necessary, reinforce these goals by listing them on a flipchart, discussing them thoroughly and pinning the flipchart up as an aide-memoire.

2. Split the participants into small teams of three or four.

3. Distribute Handouts 29.1, 29.2 and 29.3.

4. Allow the trainees two or three minutes to digest the information and find out what is expected of them.

5. Distribute Handout 29.4 and discuss this example with them – explaining that they should take a broad view in their approach to solutions.

6. Allow the participants forty-five minutes in their teams to reach a consensus and complete Handout 29.3.

Timing

With participants working in groups of three or four, this exercise usually takes about forty-five minutes to complete. A further hour should be allowed for feedback in a plenary session. Make sure that all the solutions are discussed; also emphasize the fact that many solutions can often be found to the same problem.

Materials required

1. Sufficient space for the groups to discuss their solutions, without disturbing anyone else.

2. Sufficient copies of all four handouts.

3. Flipchart listing Objectives, prepared in advance.

4. Flipchart with headings to record solutions, prepared in advance.

5. Paper and marker pens.

The manager takes stock

You are the manager of a computer services department in a public sector organization. You have been in your current post for only three months. Your family is 120 miles away in the city where you lived before gaining this post. They hope to be joining you soon – at the moment you have not been able to solve the housing problem. You have one child – a son, Marcus, aged seven. He is very worried about starting a new school and leaving his friends.

Your department has not been meeting its targets lately, mainly due to high turnover of staff. This is a great concern to you – you need to deliver a sound service as the department will be subject to a competitive tendering exercise next year. You have assessed the situation and now have an opportunity other managers never ever get.

Time has stood still – you can take stock and prepare to enjoy your 'glass of life'.

When the clock stopped there were fifteen items on your notepad – jobs you thought you needed to do. Now this heaven-sent opportunity has arrived you can set out a plan of action.

Think through the items carefully and structure your thoughts from *planning* the action right through to *delegation, doing* and *reviewing*. When deciding on your course of action, put a value on your time. Why? Because you are one of the most valuable resources your organization has.

The manager's problems

Jobs on the notepad, Thursday.

1. A member of staff, Alyssa, has been late three times this week. Her appearance is also grubby and unprofessional.

2. Your assistant manager, Mariela de Silva, is taking work home. She seems under pressure.

3. There are long delays in recruitment to your vacant posts.

4. There are long delays in attending to requests for help with computer systems.

5. Staff meetings are non-existent – all staff communication is via the notice board.

6. You have five staff appraisals to complete, but you have little objective information as you are fairly new in your post.

7. It is your partner's birthday tomorrow.

8. You have the computer suite keys. You should share this responsibility with your deputy but she never takes them!

9. No one other than your assistant seems to know the latest procedures for security of important systems.

10. Two members of staff have been smoking in a non-smoking area.

11. All managers using your department's services seem to ask to see you when other staff could well handle most enquiries.

12. Your son is playing in his first football match tomorrow.

13. There appears to be low motivation in the department generally.

14. The management team in your organization want a full review of information systems.

15. Some important new software you ordered has arrived but some of it is missing.

Solutions to the manager's problems

THE TASK	*THE CONSEQUENCES OF NOT DOING ANYTHING*	*WHAT NEEDS TO BE DONE (AND WHEN)*

Sample answer sheet

THE TASK	*THE CONSEQUENCES OF NOT DOING ANYTHING*	*WHAT NEEDS TO BE DONE (AND WHEN)*
1. Alyssa – attendance	(a) She could continue to be late. (b) Other staff could take the same approach. (c) The service quality will suffer. (d) The department's image will suffer. (e) This could impact on the competitive tendering exercise.	(a) Take her aside and ask why she is late. It may be she needs help. (By the end of next week.) (b) Explain the need for high standards of work and output. (c) Monitor future performance; give immediate feedback. (Each Friday.)

Part III
Improving team and individual performance

30

Communication charter

Description

This activity involves participants in identifying their frustrations with the communication process and agreeing a communication charter, which is to form an agreement among them.

Situations

The nature of this activity lends itself to a variety of situations. Training events focusing on communication skills, team-building skills or work ethics would benefit from its use. It can be equally effective with groups as small as four or as large as one hundred.

Objectives

- To identify the barriers to, and frustrations with, the communication process.
- To use the ideas and views of delegates to form the basic rules of communication within a unit.
- To emphasize the effect of communication on both teams and individuals.

Trainer guidance

There are no particular problems with this activity.

The best size of group to discuss a communication charter is between four and ten. This allows for up to one hundred participants in ten groups of ten.

Method

1. Begin with an open discussion about the barriers to good communication and the frustrations created by poor communication. To help the discussion at this stage give such examples as meetings, team briefings, management memos or circulars. Draw up a list of these barriers and frustrations for use later in the activity.

    Consider dividing very large groups (say, over thirty) into smaller teams to discuss this topic.

2. After identifying the barriers and frustrations, give the group(s) Handout 30.1. Explain that the participants should identify ways of overcoming the barriers and frustrations and turn these ideas into a 'Communication Charter'.

3. Give out the 'Communication Charter' (Handout 30.2) and allow the participants thirty minutes to agree their 'Top Ten Principles' To introduce a lighthearted element into the exercise, ask the groups to add a humorous eleventh item to their list.

4. In order to produce one overall charter (if there are a number of groups), nominate a spokesperson from each team to form an 'elite' group to choose the best of the items from the initial charters.

5. Produce the final draft for everyone to take away with them. Refer to the initial list of communication barriers and frustrations and restate the aim of overcoming them with the 'Communication Charter'.

Timing

Whilst the size and number of groups may vary, the timings for this exercise should not change very much. The initial discussion on the barriers and frustrations should take fifteen minutes. Each group will need thirty minutes to agree its 'Top ten' charter items. A further thirty minutes will be needed to agree the final 'Communication Charter'. Total time required approximately one hour and fifteen minutes.

Materials required

1. Sufficient study rooms for each group.
2. Sufficient copies of Handouts 30.1 and 30.2 for each group.

Communication charter

Your task

You have just identified some of the barriers to good communication and the frustrations created by poor communication.

Your group should now discuss a 'Communication Charter' designed to overcome these barriers and frustrations.

You have thirty minutes to agree your 'Top ten' and write them up on the form (Handout 30.2).

Communication charter

Top ten principles

WE SHOULD ...

1.

2.

3.

4.

5.

6.

7.

8.

9.

10.

31

From group to team

Description

This activity enables individuals and whole teams to measure their state of team development, using the concepts of forming, storming, norming and performing.

Situations

The activity can be used with whole teams as part of a team-building programme or with individuals from different teams. If complete work teams are used, it measures their present development. If individuals are from different teams, it allows feedback and discussion on the team development phases. The exercises can be used with teams of any size.

Objectives

- To help participants understand the stages of team development.
- To measure the present level of team development.

Trainer guidance

In organizations there are many collections of people which purport to be teams but are in fact groups. There is a clear distinction to be made between a group and a team which individuals often have difficulty in recognizing and verbalizing. Central to the distinction is the synergistic nature of the team when the processes operating both collectively and between individuals give rise to the 'whole being greater than the sum of the individual parts'. This hinges on two main factors: the length of time the individuals have been together and what has happened between them.

Like many other aspects of human behaviour, team-working skills can be learned and this takes time, often months or years. One cannot expect a collection of people instantly to conjure up team skills the moment they are put together. It is like asking a football team to play with orderliness and precision and win games without any practice.

This exercise uses the process of forming, storming, norming and performing in the move from being a group to being a team. It is a linear process from forming through to performing although the development process is such that any of the four stages may be utilized in a random fashion by the group, depending on the issues to be addressed. All four stages are important but of critical significance is the storming phase. This enables the relationships and procedures operating within the team to be built with greater honesty and more authenticity. Individuals express how they feel and unearth issues which are hidden and often left unsaid in many group working environments. For most groups storming is generally avoided and will not occur unless deliberately planned and carried out as part of a team-building exercise.

Method

1. Explain the purpose of the exercise. Distribute Handout 31.1 and explain to the participants the phases of team development. Show that movement is from 12 through to 12 in a clockwise direction.

2. Ask each participant to place a cross on the circumference of the circle at the point where they feel the team is in its present development state.

3. Draw the clock, with its numbers from 1 to 12 on a flipchart.

4. Ask each participant to call out the number on the clock where they have positioned their cross. Write this with a marker pen on the circumference of the clock.

5. Draw the average of the crosses and begin a discussion on the reasons for the individual and average scores.

6. Review the four stages of team development and emphasize the process required and the timescale necessary to move from being a group to being a team. Highlight the points made in the Trainer's Guidance section.

7. After a team development event, scores can be entered on the clock to measure the progress being made by the team.

Timing

1. Introducing the exercise takes five minutes.

2. Explaining the phases and individual scoring takes ten minutes.

3. Scoring on the flipchart takes fifteen minutes.

4. Discussion and concluding the exercise takes fifteen minutes.

Total average time: forty-five minutes.

Materials required

1. Sufficient copies of Handout 31.1 for each participant.

2. Flipchart, paper and marker pens.

'From group to team' clock

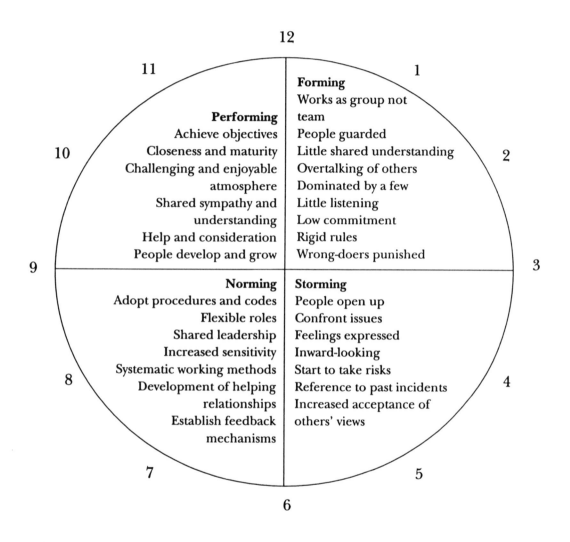

```
                          12
      11                                        1
                                    Forming
                                    Works as group not
                 Performing         team
                Achieve objectives  People guarded
                Closeness and maturity  Little shared understanding   2
  10          Challenging and enjoyable  Overtalking of others
                      atmosphere    Dominated by a few
                Shared sympathy and  Little listening
                   understanding    Low commitment
                Help and consideration  Rigid rules
                People develop and grow  Wrong-doers punished
                                                                      3
   9
                         Norming    Storming
                Adopt procedures and codes  People open up
                       Flexible roles  Confront issues
                   Shared leadership  Feelings expressed
                Increased sensitivity  Inward-looking
                Systematic working methods  Start to take risks
    8          Development of helping  Reference to past incidents    4
                     relationships   Increased acceptance of
                Establish feedback   others' views
                      mechanisms
        7                                            5
                          6
```

32

Developing team goals

Description

This activity is designed to help team members jointly to develop realistic team goals which positively contribute to organizational goals and objectives.

Situations

A productive activity in situations where teams are newly formed or have been reorganized or where members are displaying signs of confusion about team purpose. In fact, the activity can be useful in any situation where a confirmation or reaffirming of team purpose is seen to be necessary.

Suitable for use by team leaders who may decide to facilitate the process themselves or may feel the benefit of working in conjunction with an experienced trainer. In the latter case, some pre-planning would be necessary to clarify the two roles and the ways of working together on the activity.

Objectives

- To appreciate the organization's purpose and its key goals.
- To agree the team's role within the framework of the organization.
- To develop and agree team goals which will positively contribute to organizational aims and thereby enhance the team's standing within the organization.
- To consider the likely constraints in achieving the team goals.
- To review the team's capability for achieving the agreed goals.

247

Trainer guidance

These notes assume that the team leader has decided to facilitate the process. As mentioned earlier, if an experienced facilitator is to assist, agreement should be reached beforehand about respective roles.

As team leader, you should be prepared to answer questions and provide information on issues relating to organizational purpose, ethos, goals and current team directives and policies. If you prefer, you may focus on departmental or service goals. Handout 32.1 can be amended as appropriate.

Method

1. Distribute Handout 32.1 and ask each participant to spend approximately thirty minutes, either individually or in pairs, completing it.

2. Instruct the whole team to share and discuss their questionnaire responses. Their target is to reach agreement and record agreed points on to one questionnaire. This agreed statement is then presented to you as team leader.

3. As team leader you should now discuss the 'gap', if any exists, between *your* perceptions of the goals you believe your team should be pursuing and the perceptions of your team. The main purpose of this part of the process is openly to announce differences in perceptions and to work towards their reduction or removal.

4. After agreement has been reached on a consolidated view, invite the team to complete Handout 32.2. There may be advantages in your being fully involved in this stage.

5. Complete the session with an open discussion on participants' thoughts and feelings about the exercise. Ask participants to inform the group of any learning which they have gained from the activity.

Timing

1. Completing Handout 32.1 takes thirty minutes.

2. Producing agreed response to Handout 32.1 takes fifty to sixty minutes.

3. Discussion and reaching agreement on reduction or removal takes thirty-five to forty-five minutes.

4. Completing Handout 32.2 takes thirty to forty-five minutes.

5. Plenary session takes fifteen minutes.

Average total time: three hours.

Materials required

1. Sufficient copies of Handouts 32.1 and 32.2.
2. Sufficient space for participants to work undisturbed.
3. Flipchart, paper and pens.
4. Video camera and playback facilities (optional).

Developing team goals – questionnaire

1. *Organizational purpose and goals:*

   (a) What is the purpose of the organization?

   (b) What are its *key* goals?

2. *Team purpose:*

   (a) What is the purpose of your team?

   (b) Why was it formed and why does it exist now?

3. *Team vision:*

    How do you envisage your team contributing to the goals of the organization?

4. *Team goals:*

    Considering your responses to questions 1, 2 and 3, what do you consider to be your team's *key* goals?

5. Describe any problems or difficulties you experienced in developing team goals.

Team goals – notes on completing form

1. List all your team's key goals in statement form. To be complete, each goal should be clear, concise and be quantified, with a target time (where possible). For example, reduce the absentee rate to less than 1 per cent within the next six months.

2. List all the likely constraints which will hinder your team in its efforts towards the goals. For example, lack of suitable equipment.

3. List all the factors considered to be vital to success. For example good communication within the team and across team interfaces.

4. List all the skills required within the team for effective goal achievement. For example, fluency in 'business' French.

5. Indicate the team's current capability in that skill: adequate = ✓; weak = T (training required).

6. If training is required, indicate the priority of this: urgently = A; within three months = B; within twelve months = C.

7. Agree review dates when the team will meet to reflect upon goal achievement/progress/modification, etc.

Team goals

Team goals (statement)	Constraints	Factors critical to success	Skills required within the team	Capability	Priority class (A–B–C)

Review dates	1st	2nd	3rd	4th	Our capability is: adequate = ✓ weak = T (training required)	Training is required: A = urgently B: within 3 months C: within 12 months

33

Team characteristics

Description

This activity involves members of a team in working together to identify the characteristics of a good team and then rating their own team against the characteristics identified.

Situations

This exercise is suitable to use with work teams as part of a team-building event. It should be run with teams of about six participants.

Objectives

- To define the characteristics necessary for successful team working.
- To measure the team's performance against the characteristics.

Trainer guidance

The identification, understanding and use of team characteristics are vital for effective team working, for new and mature teams alike. With a new team, they serve as the foundations and guidelines to which all members refer. This not only develops a common language and understanding among the members, but also provides a means of evaluating and judging team performance. For the more mature team that is operating efficiently, team characteristics would be internalized by members and serve as operating codes and reference points for behaviour.

The process that a team goes through in identifying these characteristics is a very valuable stage of team development. Team members collectively have to think through, discuss and debate the whole issue of their team's effectiveness. This leads to a greater understanding by everyone of the features identified by teams. Many are common, for example, task achievement, sharing information and correctly diagnosing the problem. Others will be unique to the individual team, based on the characteristics of the personalities that make up the team. Team factors can change over time and they will need to be evaluated and modified as the team develops.

Method

1. Explain the purpose of the exercise and distribute a copy of Handout 33.1 to each team. Point out that the three example characteristics are given for guidance and that they are to write down their own list appropriate to their team. These have to be relevant to the tasks they are performing on the training programme.

2. From time to time, check on the progress being made and if necessary suggest characteristics from Handout 33.2.

3. When twelve characteristics have been identified and agreed, distribute Handout 33.3 and ask each member of the group to write them down in the same order.

    Stress the importance to effective team performance of team characteristics that are agreed and readily understood by all team members. Stress the points made in the Trainer Guidance section.

    A group task should now be set and on completion teams allowed to measure their performance using Handout 33.3

Timing

1. Explaining the exercise takes fifteen minutes.

2. Eliciting characteristics takes forty-five minutes.

3. Discussion and concluding the exercise takes fifteen minutes.

Total average time: one hour fifteen minutes.

Materials required

1. Sufficient copies of Handouts 33.1 and 33.3.
2. A copy of Handout 33.2 for the trainer.
3. Flipchart, paper and marker pens.

Team characteristics

BRIEFING NOTES

Operating as a team, describe and record the characteristics of a mature, effective working team. You will be using these characteristics to review your team performance in the next stages of the programme, so describe them in a positive manner in the form shown. Some examples are:

1. We achieved the task.

2. We diagnosed the problem/situation correctly.

3. We organized the leadership in response to the needs of the task.

Please write your twelve characteristics below:

  1.

  2.

  3.

  4.

  5.

  6.

  7.

  8.

  9.

10.

11.

12.

Team characteristics

TYPICAL TEAM CHARACTERISTICS

- We achieved the task.
- We diagnosed the problem/situation correctly.
- We organized the leadership in response to the needs of the task.
- We listened to each other.
- We had regular reviews of our progress.
- We encouraged the quieter members of the team to speak.
- We ensured that all ideas were evaluated.
- We set targets.
- We all contributed to the best of our ability.
- We were sensitive to each other's needs.
- We used the flipchart as a focus for all information.
- We showed unity and cohesion.
- We delegated effectively.
- We understood what we were doing.
- We had fun.
- We displayed commitment.

Team characteristics

RATING FORM

Write below the twelve characteristics that you have chosen, then rate your team's performance against them. If you agree that your team demonstrated a characteristic, rate it towards the 'Agree' end of the scale. If you disagree, give it a rating towards the other end of the scale.

Team characteristics	Disagree					Agree	
	1	2	3	4	5	6	7
1.							
2.							
3.							
4.							
5.							
6.							
7.							
8.							
9.							
10.							
11.							
12.							

34

Introducing new patterns of work

Description

This dynamic, creative activity is particularly suited to organizations which accept that all staff have views, opinions and suggestions which could lead to improvement. The activity gives participants permission to question present arrangements for work organization: it also provides a platform for participants to think creatively about the types of changes in working patterns which they believe would lead to improvements.

This activity can be approached at different levels – the total organization or the department or the section or team. It may be led by trainers or by managers/team leaders.

Situations

The reasons for undertaking the activity could be numerous. For example a team might be performing well but at the same time recognizes the need to critically examine ways of working in order to continue to perform well in a more competitive environment; a section might not be performing well and wishes to rearrange its working patterns; a department might wish to generate employees' suggestions on work patterns as an input to business planning.

Objectives

- To critically appraise current working patterns.

- To encourage members of a team or work group to develop the practice of reviewing the way they work together.

- To identify and explore alternative work patterns and weigh the benefits of these.

- To recognize participants' degree of influence in changing current working patterns and produce a plan for change.

- To present a case for changing work patterns to senior management and receive feedback together with agreement on the next steps.

Trainer guidance

You need to create an atmosphere of openness and trust when inviting participants critically to appraise current work patterns and suggest changes. The quality of data generated will depend on this. You will need to 'pave the way', reducing apprehensions and any fear of recrimination, and enabling participants to feel comfortable about sharing what they think and feel about the present order of things.

The process involves close examination of the way we do things now, even if currently successful; moving on to how we might do things differently and what would be the benefits of changing. Your role is to work towards a climate where such discussion can take place, dealing with destructive and negative behaviours and encouraging participants to think creatively about alternative ways of working.

Where the activity concerns organizational issues, you can help by setting up appropriate support and arranging for participants' suggestions to be heard by senior managers who can influence policy. You could arrange for these people to attend at the appropriate time; brief them to listen carefully to presentations; encourage them to ask questions; explain to them the importance of treating suggestions positively and being prepared to treat them as valuable data in their decision-making processes.

Method

1. Introduce the activity, emphasizing the value of candid comments and creative thinking throughout the process. As a warm-up exercise ask participants to brainstorm the following theme: patterns of work. This process should produce different perceptions of the theme and help to provide a good start to step 2.

2. Divide participants into groups: the composition of these should reflect common interest in the particular area to be pursued (that is, organizational, departmental, sectional, team or even individual). Distribute Handout 34.1 to all participants and allow some time for questions and clarification of the task to be undertaken. Ensure that everyone is clear

about the amount of time allocated for the task, and ask each group to complete it.

3. In the main group allow time for each group to present its suggestions for new patterns of working. Participants should ask questions, and give constructive criticism and feedback. Hold a debate on the advantages of proposed changes over current patterns of working.

4. Ask participants to re-form into their groups and undertake the task outlined in Handout 34.2 (for the organization approach) *or* Handout 34.3 (for the department, section or team approach).

5. Back in the main group allow time for presentations and encourage discussion and questions. Where the approach is organizational ensure any senior executives contract clearly with the group on next steps.

6. In a plenary session discuss the activity, the sharing of thoughts on the process, and the learning which participants feel they have gained.

Timing

1. Introduction and brainstorming takes twenty minutes.

2. Completing Handout 34.1 takes one hour thirty minutes to two hours.

3. Sharing suggestions and advantages of proposed changes takes thirty to forty minutes.

4. Completing Handout 34.2 or 34.3 takes thirty to forty-five minutes.

5. Presentations take sixty to ninety minutes.

6. Plenary session takes twenty to thirty minutes.

Average total time: between one half and one full day, including breaks.

Materials required

1. Sufficient copies of Handouts 34.1 and 34.2 or 34.3.

2. Sufficient space for participants to work undisturbed.

3. Flipcharts, paper and pens.

4. Video camera and playback facilities (optional)

Introducing new patterns of work

1. A critical look at current work patterns

This task provides an opportunity to review the ways in which work is done now in your organization or work area. To start your thinking you may wish to consider the following questions and add others as you progress:

- What is the purpose of our work?

- Why does the organization require our work to be done?

- How does the organization require our work to be done?

- How well is our work pattern geared to the needs of our customers (internal and external)?

- Why is our work done in the way it is?

- What forces things to be done in the way they are?

- Where and when does our work need to be done?

- What demarcation exists, and why?

- How do we behave in our work and why is this?

- How flexible are we in our work?

- How well covered are we for the unexpected?

2. Alternative patterns of work

Your group can now spend time identifying alternative ways of doing things. Ideas and suggestions should be allowed to flow freely – no matter how outlandish or bizarre they seem. You may wish to consider brainstorming to release people's thoughts on other, different ways in which your work could be organized. Another means is to consider some key questions, such as:

- If we had complete freedom how would we organize our work?

- How would we like to do our work?

- How could our work be done differently?

- What do we believe would improve it?

271

You will be able to add your own questions as you proceed: the main purpose of this stage is to generate a wide range of alternatives.

3. Choosing viable alternatives

Produce a concise statement of any criteria which would need to be met by any new or revised pattern of working. In completing this you will need to consider factors such as meeting customer needs and expectations; effective use of your resources, time, skill and knowledge, etc.

Having agreed these criteria, determine how far each of your alternative methods of working would meet them. Refine your list of alternatives to leave only those which meet *all* criteria.

4. Ranking the viable alternatives

Rank your refined list in order of preference; again you may wish to agree some criteria for doing this. For example, highest perceived benefits; appeal to customers; ease of changing; degree of personal influence in making the change; attractiveness to staff, etc.

5. Choosing areas for change

Finally, from your ranked list, choose the alternative(s) you would be prepared to invest time and energy in pursuing further. In preparation for presenting to the main group, record your chosen alternatives on flipchart paper together with the benefits which you believe would arise from the change. You will need to be clear about the advantages of your choice(s) over current working practices.

Decide how you are going to present your choices to the main group.

Preparing a presentation (organizational approach)

Prepare a presentation on new methods of working to be made to one or more senior executives who can influence organizational policy. Include in the presentation:

- Your rationale.

- Your proposed change(s) in working patterns.

- The benefits and advantages over current practices.

- Your thoughts on resource implications.

- Your suggestions for implementation.

Preparing a presentation (department/section/team approach)

Prepare a presentation, to be made to the main group, of your plan for achieving your changed working patterns. Include in the presentation:

- Specific changes to be made.
- Timescale of your plan.
- Responsibilities for implementation.
- Support and monitoring arrangements.

35

Team process analysis

Description

This activity involves team members in reflecting on aspects of team working after completing a task.

Situations

The activity is suitable for any team which wishes to strengthen joint working. It can be used as part of a team-building programme.

Objective

- To enable a team and its individual members to review their achievement and process immediately after completing a task.

Trainer guidance

Good team working has a number of clear and defined characteristics. These are important to know since they act as the guidelines for building successful teams. They also allow the team and its individual members to measure performance against them.

Frequently teams in organizations do not know why they are performing inadequately or badly. Something is not right but there are different views on what is actually wrong. Objectivity becomes caught up with emotion and perceptions of events become distorted. In these cases the factors suggested in this analysis serve as the foundations for understanding and explanation.

The team can measure their performance against the factors, thereby highlighting their strengths and weaknesses. This will also allow them collectively to plan for improvement.

The exercise should be used immediately after a team has completed a task. As preparation, draw Handout 35.1 on a flipchart before running the exercise. A team size of between four and ten participants is appropriate for this exercise.

Method

1. Explain the purpose of the exercise.

2. Distribute Handout 35.1 to each team member and ask them to focus on each factor, starting with 1. We successfully completed the task.

3. Referring to the task just completed they should individually rate their team on this factor somewhere between 1 (disagree) and 7 (agree).

4. Working individually, all the other factors should be considered and ticked until the sheet is completed.

5. Ask each team member individually to call out their rankings so that they can be recorded with a tick on the previously prepared flipchart.

6. Now analyse, looking at both the pattern of the ticks and their spread across the scale. Good team working will be shown by a close grouping of ticks on each scale and a curved pattern. Poor team working will have a wide spread of ticks and a reversed curve or random pattern.

7. Examine individual members' curves and highlight significant deviations from the team's average profile.

8. Review the points made in the Trainer Guidance section.

9. Stress that this exercise is a very useful and powerful one that can be used for any team activity, in a training session or back in the organization.

Timing

1. Introducing the exercise and completing Handout 35.1 takes five minutes.

2. Recording the individual analyses on the flipchart and discussion takes forty-five minutes.

3. Concluding the exercise with steps 8 and 9 takes ten minutes.

Total average time: one hour.

Materials required

1. Sufficient copies of Handout 35.1 for each participant.

2. Flipchart, paper and marker pens.

Team process analysis

Factor	Disagree					Agree	
	1	2	3	4	5	6	7
1. We successfully completed the task							
2. We correctly diagnosed the problem							
3. We all agreed on the approach adopted							
4. Team members listened to me when I spoke							
5. I carefully listened to all other team members							
6. I contributed as effectively as possible							
7. All other team members contributed effectively							
8. The team was dominated by one or more people							
9. Some good ideas were lost							
10. I was unhappy with my role							
11. Other members were unhappy with their roles							
12. Competition between individuals was disruptive							
13. Some members operated as though they were a team of one							

36

Postal dilemma

Description

This activity emphasizes the importance of effective communication skills, sharing information and working together in a problem-solving environment.

Situations

This activity can be used in any programme covering communication skills and team problem solving. It can be useful in team-building programmes, as a basis for reviewing the ways in which team members work together.

Objectives

- To reinforce the need for clear communication when pressed for time.

- To highlight the importance of active listening.

- To demonstrate the importance of working together to solve a problem.

Trainer guidance

The main concerns are to ensure that the rules are adhered to and to concentrate the debriefing on the key learning points by referring to specific examples.

Method

1. Divide participants into teams of six to eight (including the chairperson).

2. Give the chairperson the Brief (Handout 36.1).

3. Distribute a sealed envelope containing one of the Information Slips from Handout 36.2 to each participant. (Try to limit team numbers to six, as any additional participants will receive only blank slips.)

4. Tell the chairperson they have a maximum of thirty minutes to complete the Answer Sheet (Handout 36.3).

5. Collect the answers and name the winner.

6. Debrief the activity, relating to the points brought out, i.e. listening under pressure and clarity of communication.

Timing

The activity itself should take no longer than thirty minutes with another thirty minutes for discussion.

Materials required

1. Sufficient copies of the Chairperson's Brief (Handout 36.1).

2. Sufficient Information Slips (one per participant) in envelopes.

3. Separate rooms/areas for the teams to work in.

4. Participants' Answer Sheet – Handout 36.3 (one for each group).

5. Trainer's Answer Sheet.

Chairperson's brief

1. Each person will receive written pieces of information on slips. These must not be shown to anyone else.

2. Your aim will become clear as you share information with each other through oral communication only.

3. When you believe you have completed the exercise, inform the trainer who will tell you if you are correct. If not and time allows, try again. The trainer will not tell you which parts of your task are right and which wrong.

4. You will have thirty minutes in which to complete the exercise.

Information slips

Each participant in a team should receive an Information Slip placed in an individual envelope.

SLIP 1.
The person with the red letterbox lives next door to the house with the Austrian blinds.
Roberts has a silver letterbox.
The person who lives in the bungalow has a blue letterbox.
Only one of the houses is located on the east side of the village.

SLIP 2.
Patel's neighbour has a black letterbox.
The person who has a red letterbox also has flowered curtains.
Smith lives next door to the detached house.
One of the group's tasks is to decide who drives a Ford.
The houses in the village stand beside each other in a semi-circle.

SLIP 3.
De Silva has check curtains.
There is a BMW in the drive of the maisonette.
Each person has a different coloured letterbox.
O'Connell lives next door to Smith.
A Rover is in the garage of the terraced house.

SLIP 4.
The person with the yellow letterbox lives immediately to the east of the house with the velvet curtains.
Your group has fewer than three tasks.
The terraced house has a red letterbox.
Only one of the houses is located directly on the west side of the village.
Each of the people drives a different car.

SLIP 5.
The terraced house is in the most northerly position in the village.
Each house has different curtains.
The maisonette stands next to the semi-detached house.
O'Connell drives a Vauxhall.
Smith has a blue letterbox.

SLIP 6.
Only Smith lives at the west end of the village.
The maisonette has a silver letterbox.
One of your group's tasks is to decide who has striped curtains.
Patel lives in a terraced house.
Each person lives in a different type of house.

287

Participants' answer sheet

Names of residents	Residents' possessions				

289

Trainer's answer sheet

Trainer's material

Names of residents Residents' possessions	SMITH	O'CONNELL	PATEL	DE SILVA	ROBERTS
LETTERBOX	Blue	Yellow	Red	Black	Silver
CURTAINS	Velvet	Austrian blinds	Flowered	Check	Striped*
HOUSE	Bungalow	Detached	Terraced	Semi-detached	Maisonette
LOCATION	West	North West	North	North East	East
VEHICLE	Ford*	Vauxhall	Rover	Toyota	BMW

*Items to be deduced

Reproduced from *Activities for Public Sector Training: Achieving Change and Strengthening Teamwork*,
Gower Publishing Ltd.

37

For better or verse

Description

This activity looks at the importance of setting and assessing standards of performance through a group activity which involves setting standards for a book of poetry.

Situations

The activity is suitable for any staff who have responsibility for setting, monitoring and maintaining standards of work. The activity is especially useful for managers taking on responsibility for staff appraisal.

Objectives

- To show the importance of setting standards.
- To discuss the ways in which an employee's performance can be measured against standards.
- To evaluate the benefits of setting standards of performance.

Trainer guidance

This is a straightforward and energizing activity which should not present any problems to the trainer.

Because the activity involves group work which is not based on 'real' work it will be important to make clear links between experience gained during the group work and the working situation.

Method

1. Introduce the activity by explaining to the group that they represent a team of publishers who are planning a book of poetry, written by various poets throughout the country. The book will contain one type of poem and they, as publishers, want to set the standards for it, before asking the general public to submit their work. Standards could include:

    *   Each poem must be twelve lines long.
    *   Each line should have a minimum of nine words.

2. Split the group into two teams and ask them to produce a poem, ideally reaching the standards they set. The theme of the poem may depend on the standards of the group. It may be appropriate to encourage a poem based on a work issue.

3. Ask the teams to read their poems to each other and while this reading is taking place, ask the opposite team to rate the poem against the standards set at the start of the activity. Ask each team to discuss how they rated the poems and the reasons for these ratings.

4. Distribute Handout 37.1 and ask each group to answer the questions. Lead a discussion on the answers.

5. Point out to the group that standards can relate to a specific task or to a person's actual performance. For example, in this exercise the standards were concerned with the actual product – the poem. In another situation, as with an employee working within a customer complaints section, the standards may refer to actual performance. Use the following example to elaborate:

    *   Every written complaint should be acknowledged within two days.
    *   A response to the complaint should be given within ten days.

6. Emphasize to the group the benefits of setting standards as a fundamental management process. Ensure the following points are included:

    *   To make it clear to the employee what the organization requires.
    *   To ensure that everyone involved in a task or in delivering a service knows what to aim for.
    *   To make the process of measuring and assessing performance less subjective.
    *   To make it easier to measure and assess performance.

7. Close the activity by emphasizing to the group that as managers they need to ensure that there are standards in place for every task within the employee's job description. The employee needs to be fully briefed on these standards and understand them. It is essential that the actual performance is measured against these standards and then used within the appraisal interview and on the appraisal document.

Timing

1. Introducing the exercise and writing the standards takes fifteen minutes.

2. Producing the poem takes fifteen to twenty minutes.

3. Rating the poems and discussion takes ten minutes.

4. Completing Handout 37.1 and the final discussion takes fifteen to twenty minutes.

Total average time: fifty to sixty minutes.

Materials needed

1. Sufficient copies of Handout 37.1.

2. Flipchart, paper and marker pens.

3. Notepaper and pens.

Review of the exercise

1. What issues arose when you were producing the list of standards before writing the poem?

2. As managers, what lessons can you learn from writing this list of standards?

3. How successful were you when you measured each other's poems against the standards?

4. Why is it so important to set standards for tasks/performance?

38

Bullseye!

Description

This activity centres on the setting of objectives and action plans. First, participants look at some recommended guidelines. They then test their understanding through a practical exercise which is reviewed by linking objective setting and action plans to the appraisal process.

Situations

This activity has many uses as the guidelines for objectives and action plans apply to anyone involved in the setting of targets within the workplace.

Objectives

- To explain the theory of setting objectives and action plans using the mnemonic 'TARGET'.
- To demonstrate that the action plan is an integral part of objective setting.
- To test participants' understanding of the theory through practice and discussion.

Trainer guidance

This activity is primarily designed for use where there is a formal appraisal or performance review system. The notes on the method refer to this. The activity can be used equally well in other situations dealing with targets or performance issues. In such cases you will need to adjust your method and input to suit.

Method

1. Before the start of the activity prepare the 'Hit' and 'Miss' cards.

2. Outline the objectives of this activity to the group.

3. Lead a general discussion, opening with the question: 'Why is it so important to set objectives, especially within the appraisal process?' Ensure that the following points are included:

    - People are motivated if they have something to aim for.
    - Objectives can challenge an individual.
    - It is rewarding to reach an objective and to feel success.
    - Appraisals are not merely for the review of past performance; they are also used to guide people in the future.

4. Explain the difference between an objective and an action plan:

    - An objective is the *what* you are going to achieve.
    - An action plan is the *how* you are going to achieve the *what.*

5. Emphasize that the two go hand in hand and there are guidelines for both. Show OHP 38.1 and elaborate: an objective and action plan must be on TARGET to make it really effective. An explanation of the mnemonic follows:

    - **Testing**   What someone is aiming for should provide enough challenge to make it really testing.
    - **Achievable**   It should be challenging enough so it is almost out of reach, yet not so much that the person has little hope of achieving it.
    - **Razor sharp**   The objective and action plan should be very clear and specific.
    - **Gaugeable**   A person must be able to see very clearly how near he is to reaching the goal and be able to measure his performance at every step of the action plan and on completion.
    - **Enticing**   The goal has to appeal to the person reaching for it. Ideally it should come from the appraisee with some advice from the appraiser. This ensures commitment to the goal and the action plan.
    - **Time-related**   It is important to have a timescale attached to the objective and each element of the action plan.

Neither party is then in any doubt as to when it should be reached.

6. Distribute Handouts 38.1 and 38.2 to demonstrate that objectives can be used for both personal and work-related issues. Encourage comment and questions.

7. Introduce the next stage, telling the group that they now have fifteen minutes in which to write an objective and the associated action plan which is on TARGET. This should be work-related.

8. Critique their work with the group in the following manner, by using the 'Hit' and 'Miss' cards and by making suggestions and alterations where appropriate. Distribute one 'Hit' and 'Miss' card to each individual and request a volunteer to be the first to read their objective and action plan to the rest of the group. The others critique the objective and action plan, asking the question: 'Is it on TARGET?'

   If they believe it is, then they show the 'Hit' side of the card; if not, then they show the 'Miss' side. The volunteer may ask anyone in the group the reason for the decision on 'Hit' or 'Miss'. Continue until everyone has read their objective and action plan and it is apparent that the group understands the theory.

9. Lead a group discussion on the key points that should be considered when setting objectives within the appraisal process. Include the following:

   - Objectives should be set and agreed jointly with the appraisee. What the appraiser may perceive as achievable may not be so in the appraisee's eyes.
   - Ensure that other relevant parties are informed of the objective set. This avoids infringing on other work.
   - Objectives will naturally stem from elements of past performance that could be improved or new areas in which the appraisee would like to become involved.
   - The appraiser may have to commit to taking action to help the appraisee.
   - Objectives will need to be reviewed regularly and amended as a result of external influences such as changes in company policy.

10. Conclude the session by comparing the long-distance driver, who needs to know his destination and have a map on how to get there, with an appraisee. If appraisees do not know their target destination and have no plan of how to get there, then they are bound to get lost on the way.

Timing

1. Introduction and writing the objective takes twenty-five minutes.

2. Reading the objectives and rating them 'Hit' or 'Miss' takes approximately thirty minutes, depending on the number of participants.

3. Closing discussion takes ten to fifteen minutes.

Total average time: seventy minutes.

Materials required

1. Flipchart, paper and marker pens.

2. Overhead projector and OHP slide 38.1.

3. Sufficient copies of Handouts 38.1 and 38.2.

4. 'Hit' and 'Miss' cards. These can be made from white cards with HIT written on one side and MISS written on the other.

AN OBJECTIVE AND ACTION PLAN SHOULD BE ON:

Testing

Achievable

Razor sharp

Gaugeable

Enticing

Time-related

A personal objective

The following is an example of a personal objective and action plan that meets the TARGET criteria.

'By the end of four weeks I will have improved my fitness in the gym by 10 per cent.'

ACTION PLAN:
- To have a personal fitness test at the gym, conducted by one of the fitness instructors. The test will gauge my current fitness level. To take place this week.

- This will be followed by a recommended fitness regime, based on my requirement to improve my fitness by 10 per cent. I will take advice from the instructor as to the ability to improve my fitness by this amount within a four-week period. The timescale and/or the percentage will be adjusted accordingly.

- I will attend the gym on Monday and Wednesday evenings and Saturday mornings.

- I will wear ankle weights at home for at least one hour every day.

- I will go to the adult swimming sessions and swim at least two additional lengths each time I go. These sessions are on a Tuesday morning at 07.00.

An example of the same objective, *not on* TARGET: 'I am going to become more fit.'

A work-related objective

The following is an example of a work-related objective and action plan that meets the TARGET criteria.

'In five weeks from now I will run a training session for the department supervisors on how the internal distribution system operates.'

ACTION PLAN:
- I will spend a day with the manager at the distribution warehouse and check my knowledge of the system with him. This must take place within one week.

- Within two weeks I will organize training in those areas where I do not have sufficient knowledge.

- I will speak to the training department within the next week for advice on how to prepare for a training session.

- Within one week of the above conversation I will design the session and get feedback from the training department, making changes where appropriate.

- I will then run the training session, immediately after which I will obtain feedback from the attendees on its success.

An example of the same objective, *not on* TARGET: 'I will improve the supervisors' knowledge of the distribution system.'

39

Ghostbusters

Description

This is an activity designed to help managers and supervisors (especially those recently promoted) to be successful in those very early days by bringing a structured approach to their role.

Situations

This particular activity can be used as part of a seminar for 'recently appointed managers/supervisors' or as a 'best practice' type of activity for existing managers/supervisors. It focuses on BRAINSTORMING, COMMUNICATION and TEAMWORK.

Objectives

- To develop the skills of listening, communicating and teamwork by means of discussion.

- To highlight the need for managers to develop a creative approach to managerial behaviour.

Trainer guidance

The activity is based on the principle of the participants ridding the department/office of the GHOST of the previous manager.

This is to be done by establishing a model for BEST PRACTICE in terms of expectation management.

It is essential that the groups are *specific* in their answers and give suggestions/recommendations as to what these expectations will look like in terms of day-to-day behaviour.

Method

1. Explain the objectives of the activity.

2. Divide the participants into groups of about four.

3. Distribute the Participants' Brief (Handout 39.1).

4. Observe the groups in action.

5. Challenge the groups during the preparation stage to be specific about their expectations lists.

6. Reconvene the groups and ask each team to present their findings. Discuss and give feedback on:

   - Quality of work produced.
   - The teamwork displayed by each group.

Timing

1. Planning and preparation phase should take forty minutes.

2. Feedback takes fifteen minutes per team.

Materials required

1. Separate areas for team discussions.

2. Sufficient copies of Participants' Brief (Handout 39.1).

3. Flipchart (as required).

Participants' brief

Your task is to exorcise the *ghost* of the last manager by producing a model for BEST PRACTICE in terms of EXPECTATION MANAGEMENT.

   You are required to prepare two sets of guidelines. You have forty minutes.

Ghostbusters – expectation lists

---

1.   What expectations do you have of your staff in performance terms?

---

2.   What can they expect of you in management terms?

40

Your team leader role

Description

This activity enables participants to review their current role by working through a questionnaire and discussion.

Situations

The exercise is most suitable for first-time team leaders who are in contact with operating-type activities. The exercise can be used in groups of up to twenty participants.

Objectives

- To define four separate models of a team leader's role.

- To enable participants to determine their current team leader role.

Trainer guidance

Team leaders in the middle ranges of an organization often perform in a variety of different roles. Frequently an individual operates in a role that has developed haphazardly to fit a particular set of circumstances rather than being designed on a rational basis. It is possible to design team leader roles based on the main activities of an organization. These activities, which are listed hierarchically, are:

- **Policy making**: Usually carried out by the most senior members of management or by local authority members etc. This determines the future direction of the organization. Typical policy level decisions would include service policy and resource allocation to service areas.

- **Planning**: once policy has been set, detailed planning is often handed to the next level of management. Here, decisions are made about how policy goals are to be achieved.

- **Organizing, coordinating and controlling**: the planning stage eventually leads to action whereby decisions made about services are implemented. The function of organizing, coordinating and controlling the resources to do this often falls to the front-line team leader, manager or supervisor.

- **Operating**: finally someone has to do the work, operate the system, press the buttons, work the computer, drive the vehicle to enable the service to be delivered to the customer.

Team leaders' current activities can be examined using these four functions to see the kind of role that they are performing. The way they spend their time produces four different team leader roles:

1. **The Innovator**. Operates at the higher level of the organization, involved in policy making, planning with a little organizing, coordinating and controlling, essentially looking forward, anticipating problems and trouble-shooting.

2. **The Delegator**. Firmly placed in the planning, organizing, coordinating and controlling functions with many of the less important tasks delegated to those below.

3. **The Fire Fighter**. Organizing, coordinating and controlling but also doing operating level work. Dealing with contingencies and hiccups in the system, highly responsive with a limited view of the future.

4. **The Spare Hand**. Spends much time doing operating-level work. Difficult to distinguish between the team leader and the operatives. Very limited leader role.

By completing the questionnaire, participants are able to determine the type of role they presently perform. They are then in position to review it and make changes.

Method

1. Explain the purpose of the exercise.

2. Distribute Handout 40.1 to each participant and ask them to complete it

by allocating points between the four options to each section. Define carefully what operator work means in this type of organization.

3. Assist participants to complete the questionnaire and then distribute Handout 40.2. Help them to write in the four team leader types – Spare Hand, Fire Fighter, Delegator and Innovator.

4. Distribute Handout 40.3 and explain in detail what the four roles represent. Discuss the implications of adopting each of the roles and the effect on the team.

5. Post participants' profiles on a flipchart and discuss each in turn. Question whether individuals are satisfied with the role that they have and discuss any action they intend taking.

6. Refer to the organizational consequences of team leaders working to each of the roles and how they affect organizational culture, management and individuals.

7. Conclude by asking participants who are operating as spare hands or fire fighters how they intend to change their profile.

Timing

1. Introducing the exercise takes five minutes.

2. Completing the questionnaire and drawing profiles takes thirty minutes.

3. Posting individual profiles and discussion takes forty-five minutes.

4. Final discussion takes fifteen minutes.

Total average time: one hour thirty-five minutes.

Materials required

1. Sufficient copies of Handouts 40.1, 40.2 and 40.3.

2. Flipchart, paper and marker pens.

Your team leader role – questionnaire

Team leaders perform their jobs in a variety of different ways. It is useful for you to know the way that you operate so that you can compare your approach with that of other team leaders.

To enable you to think more clearly about your job, a number of relevant areas of the team leader's job are listed in this handout. Under each area there are four statements. From each group of four statements select the one that most nearly corresponds to your own view and assign it a 3. Select the one that corresponds least to your view and assign it a 0. For the remaining two statements assign a 2 and a 1: to the option which is nearer to your view assign 2, and to the one which is less near to your view, assign 1. For example:

Statement	View of job
5.	2
6.	3
7.	1
8.	0

It is important that you score the statements according to how you actually do your job and how you really feel about it. Frequently team leaders may wish to do their jobs in a different way but circumstances in the organization prevent them.

Operating-level work

ANSWER

1. I spend much of my time doing operating-level work. 1. . . . .
2. I spend a small amount of my time doing operating-level work. 2. . . . .
3. I only do operating-level work in an emergency. 3. . . . .
4. I never do operating-level work. 4. . . . .

View of job

5. The team leader is a high grade operative/clerical officer. 5. . . . .
6. The team leader is a working leading hand. 6. . . . .
7. The team leader position is between management and workers. 7. . . . .
8. The team leader is a full member of the management team. 8. . . . .

317

Communications

9. I am the last to know about changes that are
    taking place in my department.   9. . . . .
10. I get to know about some of the changes that are
    taking place in my department.   10. . . . .
11. I am told about most of the changes that are taking
    place in my department.   11. . . . .
12. I am involved in all the changes that are taking place
    in my department.   12. . . . .

Decision making

13. All the decisions in the department are made by
    management.   13. . . . .
14. I am involved in some of the minor decisions in the
    department.   14. . . . .
15. I am involved in most of the decisions affecting my
    department.   15. . . . .
16. I play an active part in all the decisions affecting my
    department.   16. . . . .

Delegation

17. I think the best way to get a job done is to do it
    myself.   17. . . . .
18. There are a few things I can delegate but I usually
    end up doing most of the job myself.   18. . . . .
19. I delegate some of my job but there are tasks that
    my team members cannot do.   19. . . . .
20. I delegate a great deal knowing that I can always
    trust my team to do a good job.   20. . . . .

Identification

21. Most of my friends and acquaintances at work are in
    my team.   21. . . . .
22. Most of my friends and acquaintances at work are
    my team and other team leaders.   22. . . . .
23. Most of my friends and acquaintances at work are
    team leaders and managers.   23. . . . .

24. Most of my friends and acquaintances at work are managers.   24. . . . .

Thinking and planning

25. I spend most of my time just keeping the work progressing through the section.   25. . . . .
26. I am busy all the time and get little chance to stop and think.   26. . . . .
27. I manage to think and plan ahead but it is always under pressure.   27. . . . .
28. I am able to spend sufficient time thinking and planning ahead.   28. . . . .

Your team leader role

Analysis

Copy your answers to the statements on the questionnaire into the appropriate spaces provided below. Total your scores in the boxes.

Statement Your number answer	Statement Your number answer	Statement Your number answer	Statement Your number answer
1	2	3	4 . . . .
5	6	7	8 . . . .
9	10	11	12 . . . .
13	14	15	16 . . . .
17	18	19	20 . . . .
21	22	23	24 . . . .
25	26	27	28 . . . .
Total box A:	Total box B:	Total box C:	Total box D:

Transfer the totals from boxes A, B, C, D, into the corresponding scales below, by putting an X on the appropriate point of each scale. Now draw a line to connect the Xs to produce your team leader profile.

	Box	
. . . .	A	. . . .
		0 3 6 9 12 15 18 21
. . . .	Box B	. . . .
		0 3 6 9 12 15 18 21
. . . .	Box C	. . . .
		0 3 6 9 12 15 18 21
. . . .	Box D	. . . .
		0 3 6 9 12 15 18 21

Interpretation

Your scores on the questionnaire should be interpreted in conjunction with Handout 40.3. You will see that it defines four types of team leader:

A. Spare Hand
B. Fire Fighter
C. Delegator
D. Innovator

Write the names of the four team leader roles against the A, B, C and D scales on this handout. By reading Handout 40.3, you will get a clear picture of what each type of team leader role represents.

Now examine the profile on this Handout. Your highest score represents the role that you most frequently adopt. Your second highest score shows your back-up role and so on. The lowest score represents the role that you are least likely to adopt.

This exercise is not an exact measure of your team leader role at all times. Some team leaders will fluctuate between roles depending upon their operating circumstances. It is designed to give you insights into the way you perform your job and your attitudes at work. This information can lead you to question your present approach and to make any changes you feel are necessary. It is useful to discuss the questionnaire and profile with your immediate manager who may be able to help you with any changes you wish to make.

Your team leader role – explanation

Spare Hand

There is often little to distinguish the Spare Hand team leader from other members of the team since they spend a great deal of their day doing exactly the same jobs. They step in to do the basic work of the section, department or office. Frequently one of the main reasons given for spending so much time doing this work is that the section is understaffed and so someone has to do the job.

There is usually universal acceptance by managers, team leaders and team members that it is a significant part of the leader's role to act as a spare hand. Furthermore the team leader can be quite happy performing this role since they are likely to have been team members in the past. Doing a basic teamwork task helps them to keep their hand in. It also allows them to demonstrate to team members that they still maintain the basic skills to do the job.

In this role, the team leader is little more than a leading hand, and the time spent doing basic tasks prevents them from concentrating on and managing the team as a whole. Because of the time element there is not sufficient vision and forethought given to prevent problems occurring. As a result of poor organization, they are unable to cope with the numerous contingencies that occur.

The Spare Hand team leader may be referred to as one of the management team but this often has a hollow ring to it as the main reference group is the other team members.

Fire Fighter

The Fire Fighter team leader's day is characterized by constant activity as they cope with the minute-by-minute and hour-by-hour hitches and problems which occur on the job. The Fire Fighter helps other people out of difficulties, dealing with the immediate, and is an expert at solving problems. Many of the decisions are of a short term nature, liaising with other departments, consulting other team leaders, organizing additional resources and materials and switching team members around.

Unlike the Spare Hand leader, the Fire Fighter leader would usually only do basic operating-level work in an emergency. They are the lubricant in the process of translating management's plans into action. Because of this role they are the typical 'person in the middle' being asked to implement many

of management's plans without being fully involved when they were drawn up. Management look to the Fire Fighter for loyalty and support. This often places them in conflict since they still have a very strong identity with their team. Often they can be short-circuited by trade union representatives and would not be included in management–union negotiations.

Because they deal almost exclusively with everyday problems Fire Fighters lack the ability to look ahead, to reflect on matters and to anticipate problems. Their management approach lacks a future perspective.

Delegator

This is the role management desires for their team leaders. The correct balance has been achieved between the planning and organizing, coordinating and controlling aspects of the job. Team leaders in the Delegator role are frequently much more involved with management in aspects of planning than their Fire Fighter colleagues. They are one step back from the day-to-day running of their section or department which they control through delegating the simpler tasks to team members.

It is also likely that they will have developed a system of communication and management controls which makes their job of managing much easier. Involvement and close association with management in the planning function allows them to develop a wider perspective and also brings to their attention important information and relevant factors that colleagues working at lower levels do not possess.

It is likely that the Delegator will have much closer identification with management than either the Spare Hand or Fire Fighter and is quite likely to insist they are a member of the management team.

Team leaders only become Delegators as a result of a direct management policy. Those chosen to be team leaders should be capable of exercising management skills, and management must encourage them to use those skills. Too few team leaders operate as Delegators, yet many team leader training courses assume that they do.

Innovator

It is unlikely that the Innovator team leader would have evolved from conventional management thinking about the role of the team leader. Organizations which have this type of team leader role probably have a management philosophy of job development and are likely to have been involved in a number of initiatives using these principles.

They would have given the work group as much authority, responsibility and discretion as the day-to-day running of the job would allow and would have removed many of the fire fighting, organizing, coordinating and

324

controlling tasks from the team leader. Tasks such as organizing work rotas, assigning overtime, agreeing output targets, monitoring quality standards, training staff, selecting new team members would, where possible, be the responsibility of the work group.

The new role would be that of team leader, resource controller and link with senior management. For these tasks team leaders would need a broad range of skills and knowledge, not only supervisory and managerial, but also product and technical. This would enable them to become involved in policy-level decisions that affected their section, such as the purchase of new equipment and machinery, the introduction of new services and changes in services, payment methods and employee relations policy. Similarly they would have a significant input into such aspects as material specifications, organization of maintenance, work flow from other departments and liaison with service departments.

The Innovator team leader would be specially selected and would be a high status member of the management group with the rewards of such an important position.

Appendixes

A

Questions I'd like to ask

This activity is an effective *ice-breaker*, to be used as part of the introduction to a training course. It is particularly useful where the participants are not too familiar with each other.

Objectives

- To break down any initial barriers individuals may have before the 'teaching' sessions begin.

- To help the participants to get to know each other better.

Trainer guidance

None.

Method

1. As part of the Introductory session of a training course,

    (i)   Pair the participants up.
    (ii) Give the individuals five minutes to make a list of 'Questions I'd like to ask' about their 'partner' which they feel would interest the group as a whole. No talking is allowed.

2. Allow them two minutes to ask their questions.

3. Allocate each individual one minute to tell the group what they have managed to discover about the other person.

Timing

1.   The preparation phase for the questions takes five minutes.

2.   The 'asking and finding out' section takes two minutes.

3.   The 'revelation' period is one minute per person.

Materials required

None.

B

Activity appraisal

This activity, or a modified version of it, can be used after any exercise which requires an assessment of how the task has been performed and which also requires the appraisal to be participant-centred.

Objectives

- To assess performance in terms of task, process, attitude and/or relationships.

- To enable the participants to take control of the appraisal rather than to rely on the trainer.

Method

1. Immediately after the end of an activity, give the participants a few minutes' free time to wind down, to chat amongst themselves and thus start the process of mutual appraisal.

2. Describe the need for and process of appraisal, evaluation and assessment of what has been done so that the maximum amount of learning can be extracted from the experience. (At this stage, if you consider it relevant and it has not already been described, deliver a mini-session on Kolb's Learning Cycle.)

3. Issue the Activity Appraisal Handout (pp. 335–37) and ask the participants to write down on the sheet short descriptions of their views, opinions, thoughts and feelings as these apply to the questions posed. This stage of the exercise should be undertaken as individuals.

331

4. When all the participants have made some entries on the sheets, invite them to share their views with the group as openly as they feel they can. Invite them also to take responsibility for the appraisal in that you, the trainer, place no constraints on them (other than that of time, if appropriate). Consequently, how they perform the appraisal and to what level, etc., is completely in their hands, and all that you ask of them is that they answer all the guideline questions on the sheet.

5. Clarify with the group the role they wish you to take. Remind them that you have observed their performance of the task and as such may have seen and heard things of which others were unaware. However, you will enter the appraisal only on their invitation and to the extent that they decide. If the participants do decide to include you, permanently or intermittently, you must ensure that your contributions are the minimum necessary; otherwise there is the danger that you may (unwittingly) take over the discussion.

6. During the following discussion and appraisal, the participants may wish to keep the discussion at an oral level. Or you may choose to tell them before any discussion begins that one way of easing the transition is for

   (i) the guidelines to be written on several sheets of newsprint/ flipchart paper and posted on the training room walls; or
   (ii) each participant to write on the guideline sheets so posted words or short phrases reflecting what they have written on their personal sheets.

   The entries on the posted sheets will then act as an introduction to the discussion, and can be retained by the group as a record to be compared with appraisals later in the course.

Timing

There are four options:

- The trainer imposes a time control because of the needs of the remainder of the course.

- The trainer imposes no time constraints so that the discussion can continue as long as necessary.

- The participants can impose their own arbitrary time constraint.

- The participants decide to allow the activity to run its natural course.

Materials required

1. Copies of the Activity Appraisal Handout for each participant.
2. Supplies of newsprint/flipchart paper and marker pens.
3. A supply of a reusable adhesive such as Blu-Tack.

Activity appraisal

1. How successfully was the task performed? How was it performed? Were you satisfied with the outcomes?

2. What were the main reasons for the success or failure (or something in between)?

3. Were ideas listened to? Whose?

4. How were decisions made? By whom?

5. How much listening was taking place? Did *you* listen? Were *you* listened to?

6. What was the extent of the participation of the individuals in the group? Did some have too much to say, have too large a share of the time available? Were some too quiet, or even completely silent, and make too small a contribution both to the time allocation and value within the task?

7. Did the quieter ones gain as much from their activity as the more active ones? Who says so – the quiet ones themselves or the others?

8. What was the level of support within the group?

9. What 'undesirable' behaviour occurred? (Arguing, sarcasm, put-downs, ignoring, opting out etc.)

10. What have you learned   (a) from the activity being appraised?
                             (b) from this appraisal?

11. Which question was the most difficult to answer

     (a)   in the activity (if appropriate)?
     (b)   in this appraisal?

     Why?